Treasures
for the
Heart

Lex Adams

Spirit of Truth Publications
P.O. Box 2979
Minden, NV 89423

Treasures for the Heart

Published by Spirit of Truth Publications
P.O. Box 2979
Minden, NV 89423

International Standard Book Number 0-9643206-0-6

All Scripture references are from the King James Bible

This book is dedicated to my loving and supportive family: my parents, my wife and my children who in their individual ways have helped me along life's path.

CONTENTS

INTRODUCTION

Treasures for the Heart is a compilation of periodical writings with each chapter standing alone as a meditative look at various portions of the Bible. With chapters addressing encouragement for the heart, faith, Christian maturity, and yielding to the Lord, the book touches on many different needs for the believer today. To receive the maximum benefit from each portion, allow time to prayerfully consider the message. Study the Scriptures referenced and allow God to quicken His truth in your heart. The Holy Spirit is the teacher, and as your eyes are upon Him, He will surely enlighten and minister far beyond the printed page.

Chapters 17-24 address the inner work of God in our hearts through the principle of the cross. They speak to the work of the cross from various perspectives. Because they address the same subject with different points of emphasis, I recommend reading them separately, over time, rather than at one sitting. The cross is not only a Christian symbol in remembrance of Jesus, but is also a spiritual principle, that the Holy Spirit desires to apply to our hearts. It is a central theme in the Gospel message. The clarity of our own hearts shades our perception of God and His truth. As a prism deflects light, so our hearts interpret God to the level of our understanding. We see Him more clearly, through the loving and persistent work of God in our hearts, as He uses the principle of the cross. The treasures of truth reflect more beautifully and accurately through us, as we yield to His Spirit. It was through Jesus' crucifixion and death that He experienced the resurrection. His resurrection power and light transform our lives, as we yield to the precious work of the cross in our hearts.

Chapter 16, "There is a Second Death," addresses the nonbeliever, while the rest of the book addresses a Christian audience. I include this chapter, because I do not know who may read this book. If one soul comes to know Jesus as their Savior, then we will all rejoice together.

Jesus tells us that where our treasure is, there will our hearts be also. May these pages help in some way to make heaven, and the things of God, our most valued and sought after treasure.

1

"AND JESUS STOOD STILL AND COMMANDED HIM TO BE CALLED."
Mark 10:49

Heavenly Father, once again we come to You bringing every care and concern. We are privileged that through the name of Jesus we are granted an audience at the very highest throne of all power and authority. This is amazing to us, as we realize that He who created all things has committed to listen to our petitions, because we approach Your throne in the name of Your Son, Jesus. Thank You for Your great compassion toward us. Praise be unto You, for You are a glorious God. Let us learn to worship You in the beauty of holiness, for our relationship withYou is a sacred thing to be cherished. In Jesus' name we pray.

Faith is a marvelous and mysterious thing. How it works and how it connects us with God is really unexplainable. Somehow, something within the heart of man becomes alive, quickened by the Holy Spirit of God. Faith is not a mental frame of mind. It is a reality of the heart given by God to those who believe. The most beautiful thing about faith is how God reacts to it and receives it. Faith definitely connects the heart of man with the power of God, and the results are something very special.

People with quickened Holy Ghost faith are compelled into action. Four men, who knew a severely crippled man, had heard that Jesus was in a home in their city. They purposed to take their friend to Him. They carried him across town on a stretcher to the location of Jesus. Upon arriving at the home, the crowd was so great that they could not get him inside. However, this thing called faith pressed them forward. They had to get the crippled man to Jesus. So they proceeded to tear apart the roof of the house. Once a hole was made, they lowered their friend into the home near Jesus. Faith had overpowered them. They knew that they must get this man to Jesus. They refused to be turned away by the crowd. A short time later, this man was walking home praising God for His mercy and healing. We read that "When Jesus saw their faith" he began to minister to the man, first proclaiming that his sins were forgiven and next causing him to walk. This is the wonderful response of God to true Holy Ghost faith (Mark 2:1-12).

In Matt. 15 we read an extraordinary story of a woman's faith. She was not a Jew, not one unto whom Jesus was at this time sent to minister. But she had heard of Him. She believed in Him and she came to Him. She asked Him to deliver her daughter from a devil. Jesus did not answer at first, but was silent. She persisted in her plea until the disciples of Jesus came and asked Him to send her away because of her annoying crying. He then explained that He was not sent to minister except to the children of Israel. When she heard this, she refused to accept His answer. Bowing at His feet, she continued to worship Him and requested His help. He however, again responded that it was not proper for Him to take that which was purposed for the children of Israel and give it unto dogs. Quite a humiliating statement to the woman. Perhaps she thought of herself as worthy in a wrong way and this was Jesus' way of humbling her. God only knows what He was working in this woman's heart, but in the face of this comment she yet persisted and stated, "Truth Lord, yet the dogs eat of the crumbs which fall from their masters' table." She pleaded, "Master, yes, though I be only a dog in comparison to Israel, yet I plead with Thee for but a crumb from Thy table...just one crumb." Jesus, at this, could not resist her faith. He could not turn away. He would not turn away! He looked at this woman, saw her persistent faith and said to her, "O woman, great is thy faith: be it unto thee even as thou wilt." Faith was so alive in this woman that she could not turn away from seeking Jesus. It consumed her...it propelled her...it humbled her...it connected her with God and she had to continue until she heard from Him. This is true Holy Ghost faith.

Bartimaeus was a blind man, who would sit along the road outside the city of Jericho, and beg for a living. He had heard about Jesus. One day as he was sitting by the road, there was a commotion as a great many people began passing by that way. Bartimaeus was blind, but he could hear well, and he heard that it was Jesus who passed his way with many people following Him. Realizing in his heart that Jesus could heal his eyes, and knowing it beyond any shadow of a doubt, he began to cry aloud. "Jesus, thou son of David, have mercy on me." Many around him, more than one, admonished him to "be quiet beggar...hold your peace." But something was alive in this man. Something more powerful than himself. A hope had been quickened at the hearing of the nearness of Jesus, and he began to cry aloud all the more. "Jesus, Thou son of David, have mercy on me." In the middle of the crowd Jesus stopped and stood still. Whether he heard Bartimaeus with His natural ears, or whether He heard the calling of faith, I do not know. We do know that Jesus stood still. He would go no farther. He had heard a call of faith from the heart of Bartimaeus. Jesus commanded that Bartimaeus be brought

11

to Him, and asked him what he wanted from the Lord. Moments later Bartimaeus, with sight fully restored, was one of the multitude that proceeded out of Jericho, following Jesus (Mark 10:46-52).

The scriptures are full of many more stories of faith alive and vibrant in the hearts of men and women who were so moved and focused on the Lord, that they would not be turned away until they had touched Him. In Mark 5 a ruler of the synagogue came to Him...and a common woman with an issue of blood was healed. The picture is clear, Jesus responded to faith. Whether faith was in the ruler of the synagogue, a Gentile woman, a poor blind beggar, a soldier or a priest, Jesus would not pass them by. When He heard the call of faith He stopped, stood still and took the time to minister to each one. He was drawn to faith, true active Holy Ghost heart level faith. It didn't matter what the status of the person was, where faith was active, Jesus was there. He is no respecter of persons.

Lord, grant unto each one who needs Your help, for whatever reason, a quickening of faith to receive from Your gracious and compassionate hand that for which he prays. Let us see through faith, that the throne to which we come is that of the Almighty. There is nothing, absolutely nothing, that is too hard for You or impossible with God. Let this be the foundation for all of our prayers and our approach to all of life's challenges. Precious Jesus, it is in Your name we pray. A-men.

2

"THOU GOD SEEST ME"
Gen. 16:13

Heavenly Father, we know that You take notice of even the smallest things in our lives and care about each of them. We thank You that You are never too busy to listen to our prayers; never too far away from us to draw near when we call upon You; never too superior to be burdened with our needs. Your willingness to be involved with us is a testimony of Your greatness and of Your great love for us. Thank You for Your caring and watchful eye which seeks to preserve us from darkness and turn each challenge into an opportunity to know more of You. We praise You and bow before You with grateful hearts. In Jesus' name we pray.

In our affliction, trials, seeking of God, times of blessing and the common activities of life, we can be assured that God sees us and beholds our situation. We can take encouragement from Scripture and the testimonies of others that even when it seems things are too much to bear, God is near and ready to help.

In Genesis 16, Hagar was mistreated by Sarai. So bad was the treatment that Hagar ran away into the wilderness. She sought to escape a very difficult situation. Lo and behold, no sooner had she fled than an angel of the Lord met her and communed with her. He asked her, where did you come from and where will you go? She explained her flight, but did not answer of where she would go. It is not told us in Scripture, but we assume that she had not thought of where she would go, but had only thought of the immediate desire to flee. This reaction is not uncommon when pressures of trials and adversity touch our lives. We often think to "flee" with little or no thought of the consequences or of "where we will go." The angel told Hagar that God had heard her affliction. That in itself was a great relief and comfort. (From this knowledge alone we can gather much strength. God knows of my affliction! I am not without Him in this situation! This is refreshing for the soul.) The angel then told Hagar to return to Sarai and submit to her. There was more to be accomplished in this situation and Hagar was to be a part of what was developing. With the strength and comfort of knowing that God had seen her affliction, she returned.

In Acts chapter 8, we read of a high ranking Ethiopian official of great authority (who served under Candace, the queen of Ethiopia) who was returning from Jerusalem. He had gone there to worship. He had taken a long journey from Ethiopia for the sole purpose of worshipping God. He was a seeker of God, and was now returning to his home and was reading the book of Isaiah (Esaias) in his chariot. God had seen this man. He had watched as he left Ethiopia to come to worship. God saw his spiritual hunger and was very aware of this one lone person traveling in the desert. God spoke to Philip and commanded him to go out into the desert as you go from Jerusalem to Gaza, and so Philip went. He saw the Ethiopian's chariot and the Lord told Philip to go up to the chariot. As he approached he heard the man reading the book of Isaiah aloud. As Philip and the Ethiopian spoke about Isaiah's words, the Ethiopian opened his heart to the message of the Lord Jesus, received Christ as his Saviour, and was baptized. This Ethiopian returned home a new creature in Christ and rejoicing in how God had met him and revealed Himself unto him. God beheld this one lone individual and his desire for God, and God did not fail to reach out and touch him.

In Acts chapter 10 we read of a Roman soldier, a centurion or captain over 100 soldiers. This soldier endeavored to live a life seeking God. We are told that he prayed always and gave assistance to many people. Here he was, living his life as a soldier in the Roman army, praying and doing good to help those around him. Unknown to him, God had been keeping a record of this man Cornelius. God knew of all his prayers and of all his giving. One day in a vision God tells Cornelius, "Thy prayers and thine alms are come up for a memorial before God." Something as simple as regular prayers and giving had come to be a memorial before God. God had seen this man. God had not ignored his dedication but had kept a record of it! Peter is then sent to Cornelius' house and as he is speaking about Jesus, the entire group is filled with the Holy Spirit. Salvation and the baptism of the Holy Spirit had come to Cornelius' home because of his seeking of God.

These are tremendous stories of God's watchful and caring eye overseeing each one who seeks Him. Whether in adversity, or in the routine of daily life, God does see. God does care, and He does draw near to those who suffer and who seek Him diligently. There was nothing fancy about Cornelius' life or walk with God. There was nothing spectacular about the Ethiopian's seeking of God. There was only a true desire and hunger for Him, and God moved to meet that hunger. His love reaches out to the one…to the individual…to you and to me.

Thank You, Lord, for Your tender and caring love for us and for Your ever present help. Nothing touches us of

15

which You are not aware, and nothing can harm us, for You are with us in all of life's experiences.

3

"THE LOVE OF THE TRUTH"
II Thes. 2:10

Heavenly Father, we are grateful for Your care and concern toward us. We are thankful for Your provision and blessings in our lives. In adversity we are thankful for our faith in You, which helps us to see beyond the difficult moments. Though it may seem at times that adversity will never yield, we claim Your victory. In the times when we lack a complete understanding of 'why', let us learn to rest in the promises of Your word and the comfort of Your presence. With grateful hearts we praise You. In Jesus' name we pray.

Power! Signs! Wonders! As told in II Thes. 2:9-10, all of this can be the partner of unrighteousness, deceit and Satan. Things that appeared great but were not. Things that appeared religious but were not of God. Elsewhere in Scripture we see power, signs and wonders at the hands of Jesus. Things that appeared good and were. Things that appeared to be of the Spirit of God and were of God. We know that we are admonished to try the spirits to determine whether they are of God (I John 4:1). This we must do to not be deceived. And further, we are shown an important ingredient to that which is of God…"the love of the truth." II Thes. 2:10 states that those who believed the lie did so because they had not received the love of the truth. This is the "agape" of the truth, God's love.

The love of the truth is not knowledge of the Word alone.

It is not the adherence to religious procedures or an impressive attendance record. The "agape" of the truth, the core of intention from God, is the fact that God loves me as a sinner. This is what one must receive to begin to know truth in the spirit and not be deceived. One must admit his sinful state. One must see God's great unconditional love as the source of sin's forgiveness and receive it. Jesus' sacrifice, shed blood and resurrection are the proof of this love. If we reject this, we reject any real understanding of God.

How wonderful to think that God requires only that we receive the love of the truth. We are not worthy; we cannot work to become worthy; He asks only that we receive His love - the love of the truth. The love of the truth is the purpose of the truth, which is that we might be saved from sin, condemnation and eternal torment. God's purpose in the truth is that we might have fellowship with Him. How wonderful and simple. He loves me as I am and asks that I believe in this love, that I might receive His great promises.

Those who have received this love rest in the knowledge that "God loves me and I belong to Him." Come what may, we are at peace in this love of God. Remembering that the purpose of God's love is salvation and eternal life, we then should not fear. To the degree that we have fear we are not fully resting in the love of God. I John 4:18 says, "There is no fear in love; but perfect love casteth out fear: because fear hath torment. He that feareth is not made perfect in love." Fear of tomorrow paralyzes us today. Fear is a robber and a thief, taking from us today's joys and blessings. Fear shrouds us from God's love and the love of those around us. Fear and its accompanying torment are from the evil one, not from God.

No one is given to know the things of tomorrow. We

must learn to rest in God's love in the *now* of His presence and not let the enemy rob us of our joy. If we remember God's intention, which is our salvation and eternal life with Him, we should allow no place for fear. Our destiny is sealed and secure. Storms may blow across our bow, and storm clouds may gather overhead, but there is no power that can change the promises and intentions of God concerning our souls' salvation and eternal destiny with Jesus.

We must receive the love of the truth to be saved. Truth can be studied and configured in many forms, but to receive its love requires repentance and a confession of our sins. Without this we are left with a concept that is void of God, for God is love (I John 4:8). As we abide in His love, we will know the true signs of God.

4

"WHO HATH ENABLED ME"
I Timothy 1:12

Heavenly Father, how precious and wonderful is Your love toward us. Such a privilege it is to search out Your truths and to be taught by the Holy Spirit. Such a friend and comforter we have in Him who was sent to be with us until Jesus' glorious return. You are a sacred and holy God, may we approach you as such, and may our lives not bring reproach upon You in any way. For You have granted that we should bear Your name. Lord, let us not fail to seek to please You and You alone. May we more identify with being crucified with Christ that You may live through us less hindered by self. In Jesus' name we pray.

How well Paul knew of what he spoke! Being enabled (empowered) for God's work by Jesus, Paul thought it quite amazing, that from a background of utter defiance and hatred for the followers of Jesus, he now was in the Lord's service. Paul gratefully says, "I thank Christ Jesus our Lord, who hath enabled me, for that he counted me faithful, putting me into the ministry; who was before a blasphemer, and a persecutor, and injurious." Even though miracles were wrought through the hands of Paul, yet he considered himself "chief among sinners" (I Tim. 1:15). In Paul's words we can feel the deep emotion, appreciation, and humility as he says, "enabled ME...counted ME faithful...putting ME into the ministry." Me of all people; me who consented to the death of Stephen (Acts 8:1); me who persecuted the church (Acts 8:1-3; 9:1-2); me who thought that I was walking pleasing before God after the manner of the fathers (Phil. 3:4-6; Acts 22:3-4); me of all men he enabled, counted faithful and put into the ministry!

In I Cor. 15:9 when Paul states, "For I am the least of the apostles, that am not meet to be called an apostle, because I persecuted the church of God," he was not making a false statement of humility. Paul, from the bottom of his heart, felt it was an amazing act of God's grace to allow him to be in the ministry after so violently persecuting the Lord's people. He meant it when he said he was the least. He meant it when he said he wasn't fit for the privileged calling. And indeed for any sinner to be saved by the grace of God, it is equally a privileged calling. To think that we who were in our sinful nature, disobedient to God and dead in our sins, should have the very special privilege of being forgiven of our sins and promised eternal life in the Kingdom of God, is certainly worthy of our deepest heart felt gratitude!

There is a sacred beauty to the discovery Paul made that caused him to say "Christ Jesus...enabled me." Before Paul saw this beauty and learned of the enabling of the Holy Spirit, he first saw how useless were his own talents and credentials of themselves. On his way to Damascus, Paul was confident in his Jewish heritage, his following of the Pharisees' beliefs, the teaching of Gamaliel (who was held in great respect among the people, under whom Paul had studied… Acts 5:34 & 22:3), and confident in his following of the law (Phil.3:4-6). In an instant, this confidence perished as Paul came face to face with Jesus and the power of the Holy Spirit (Acts 9). Paul clearly learned the difference between reliance upon self and reliance upon the person of the Holy Spirit. From that moment, Paul craved to know only Jesus and His power, and to trust in Him.

Paul paid a tremendous price of sacrifice to learn of the ways of the Spirit. In Paul's own words he says, "I am crucified with Christ" and "I die daily." He saw so precisely that only through the Holy Spirit could he be effective in ministry, that he actually cherished the loss of all things and welcomed the sacrifices, for they brought him closer to Jesus and into a greater understanding of the ways of the Holy Spirit. For we read in Phil. 3, "What things were gain to me, those I counted loss for Christ. Yea doubtless, and I count all things but loss for the excellency of the knowledge of Christ Jesus my Lord: for whom I have suffered the loss of all things, and do count them but dung, that I may win Christ."

So real to Paul were the things of the Spirit, that in spite of all he suffered from beatings, prison, and persecutions, he thanked Christ Jesus for putting him into the ministry. He did this without hesitation ("Yea doubtless"). Paul had discovered something so precious, so sacred and so very special that all of life's experiences and riches could not for one moment entice Paul, for he had found Jesus and He was very real to Paul.

The enabling of God is a glorious and wonderful thing. It is likened unto a treasure chest full of every tool and every piece of equipment necessary for the job at hand. And the provisions of the Holy Spirit (through His enabling) are perfectly fitted to the task, absolutely perfectly fitted. But these "tools" are not accessible to man in the flesh. They are opened only unto the Holy Spirit. And the Holy Spirit utilizes vessels, enabling them with these very special and perfectly fitted tools. Vessels who have "suffered the loss of all things." Those who have been "crucified with Christ!" What are these "tools?" The gifts of the Holy Spirit. The power of the Holy Spirit! The wisdom and knowledge of the Holy Spirit! The love and compassion of the Holy Spirit! Paul knew about them, and they were so precious to him that everything else was but "dung."

When someone has been enabled by the Holy Spirit for the work of God, that one will always speak reverently about the Father, the Son and the Holy Spirit. That one will always give God the glory and will stand with Paul in saying from the bottom of the heart, "I am not worthy to be called by His glorious name...for I am but a sinner saved by His grace." When people are enabled by the Holy Spirit they see God as He is: holy, sacred, full of glory and compassion, and their work will reflect this great reverence for the things of God.

Blessed Jesus, bring us to the place of understanding how precious is Your enabling, how holy is Your calling and how sacred is the work of the Holy Spirit. May we learn not to grieve Him and to better follow Him each moment of our lives.

5

THROUGH THE EYES OF A PROPHET
II Kings 6:17

Heavenly Father, we are grateful for the Holy Spirit who abides with us daily through this life. We thank You for His teaching, for His guidance and help in every situation. We thank You for the strength and encouragement of Your Word, which feeds our spirits and girds us with hope regardless of the circumstance. We thank you for the sacrifice of Jesus on the cross, for the shedding of His blood which cleanses our sins and grants us access into Your most holy presence. Let us learn to show You the reverence and respect due Your name. Teach us these things as we enter the inner sanctuary of worship and behold You in Your glory and majesty. In Jesus' name we pray.

Elisha was a mighty prophet of God. In reading glimpses of his life we are enlightened into seeing in the realm of the Spirit. This realm of faith looks beyond the appearance of things in this world and beholds God. Through the life of the prophet, God is beheld by the prophet and revealed unto many. Only what is beheld is revealed, for we can only share with others that which we ourselves have experienced and learned first hand. This is the type of sharing that results in the manifestation of God, to the degree that we have experienced Him.

In II Kings 4 a poor widow is helped because of a miracle. With one pot of oil, many empty vessels were filled to supply her need. This was not possible in the natural. The oil in the one container would have filled only a similar vessel, but in this case the oil kept flowing until many more were filled. Elisha gave these instructions because he was seeing in the realm of God; the realm that truly is the final authority in all things. Elisha had traveled with Elijah and had beheld the power of God through him. Perhaps this helped Elisha to know that such things were possible. As we read of His power in the Bible and claim the Word as absolute truth, we gain a foundation for faith. The more we behold His power in the Word, God causes our faith to rise.

To the one who sees as the prophet does, in the realm of God, what appears in the natural is not the final authority. The laws of nature, science and the physical realm are subject to the power of God. By the person of the Holy Spirit, God affects and changes things in the natural realm. Such acts of God give us a glimpse of the Kingdom which is soon to come. We do not now see all, but partially. Even those mightily used of God such as Elisha and Paul proclaimed that they knew only in part. None of us knows everything. In II Kings 4:27 Elisha says, "the Lord hath hid it from me, and hath not told me." Paul states in I Corinthians 13:12, "now we see through a glass, darkly; but then face to face: now I know in part; but then shall I know even as also I am known." We know only that which we are given to know. It is nothing to boast about, for knowledge of the things of God is a gift from the revelations of the Holy Spirit. We have done nothing to obtain understanding, it is given to us by God. Not given to glorify the one receiving, but to glorify God (I Cor.4:7).

All that we learn is given to be used by the Holy Spirit for God's glory, not for the glory of the one used. In II Kings 5 we read the story of the healing of a leper named Naaman, who was a mighty captain of the host of Syria. As the story unfolds, this great captain comes to Elisha expecting him to perform some great deed or dramatic approach to healing. Elisha doesn't even come out of his house, but sends word of what Naaman is to do. Following the final compliance by Naaman, he is healed and returns to see Elisha. His words at that time were not praise for Elisha, but for God. "Now I know that there is no God in all the earth, but in Israel." Here we see God, through the power of the Spirit, glorify Himself. The prophet was merely being an obedient vessel. Elisha could have used the revelation for his own glory and gain, but he refused. Such is the way God wishes us to use that which He gives.

Through Elisha we see God's healing power; we see the dead raised as told in II Kings 4; we see an entire army in pursuit of Elisha single-handedly led captive by him in chapter 6, and the power awaiting in the realm of the spirit is revealed to us as an army of chariots of fire are shown to Elisha (II Kings 6:17). This same power is here today. It is through faith awakened, and yielding the life completely to Him, that we begin to see glimpses of such things. Faith opens our eyes into the realm of the "all things possible." Such understanding and faith are not given for us to control, but rather are given to provide God the opportunity to manifest and glorify Himself. We are not to use the things of the Spirit, but rather are to be used by the Spirit. There is a great difference. Elisha shows us how to be used by the Spirit, and refuse to use the things of the Spirit incorrectly.

Elisha saw, believed and acted. Many beheld the results but few pursued such a deeper relationship. Even among the prophets and their families we see in II Kings 6 that when the axe head fell into the river, it wasn't one of the sons of the prophets that believed to retrieve it, but Elisha. Somehow he was connected enough in the realm of the Spirit to not let the natural laws limit his faith in God. Many may believe in God, but fewer are connected enough to act on their faith. Jesus encourages us to become those who act. In John 14:12 we read, "He that believeth on me, the works that I do shall he do also; and greater works than these shall he do."

The door is open to anyone who wishes to pay the price to follow Jesus. The more submission, the more sacrifice, the more death to self-will, the more one is prepared to be used of the Holy Spirit. Knowledge and belief without the foregoing leads more toward using the things of God, not being used of God.

Faith says, "I accept nothing in the natural as final or lim-iting; not cancer...not brain damage...not unbelief in one for whom we pray...not famine...not death...not an army of the enemy at the gates...not poverty." Elisha was not lim-ited by any of these and neither should we be. Faith says, "It may be there in the natural but I'm looking up...I see something beyond and something greater." Faith says, "I will pray...I will believe...I will trust in and wait upon the Lord." The greater clarity we have in understanding our own absolute helplessness, the better position we are in to see faith rise and God be manifest.

God's work in the heart makes us know that we can do nothing of His work...that we can offer not one good thing of ourselves...not one word...not one prayer...not one song that will bless unless He fills them with His Holy Spirit. In the realization of our helplessness faith rises to say, "But with God all things are possible". In II Kings 6 & 7 we read the dreadful story of a war and famine so bad that women were killing their own children for food. Through the word of the Lord, Elisha proclaimed that in one day the situation would totally turn into that of plenty. How could he say such a thing? In the natural it was impossible. He could say it because he knew in Whom he had believed and saw in the realm of the Spirit. God can do the same for us. Regardless of what challenges we may face in our lives, may God bring us into prayer and the deeper sanctuaries of worship until we begin to see Him and all things, through the eyes of the prophet, the eyes of the Holy Spirit.

6

"AFTER THIS MANNER THEREFORE PRAY YE..."
Matt. 6:9

Heavenly Father, we have so much yet to learn and understand. We thank You for Your patience and for Your constant comfort in times of distress and challenge. We are bent toward *doing* more than toward *yielding*. Our activity covers over our inner needs, and they remain unsatisfied until we pause to reflect upon You. Our rushing to and fro masks our inner weakness and pain. Teach us to sit at Your feet that we might be healed in the inner parts of our being. Grant that we might learn more of Your ways and become more like You; not becoming more active for the sake of doing, but being filled with more of Your love and grace. In Jesus' name we pray.

The passages which follow are often referred to as the Lord's Prayer. What they represent is more of an instruction in prayer as Jesus was teaching His disciples. In Luke 11, we find Jesus responding to a request from His disciples to be taught how to pray. It is worth pondering this instruction in prayer as it reveals many things beneficial to our prayer life.

"Our Father, which art in heaven." Here Jesus leads us to know Who we are addressing in prayer and where He abides. He is "our Father." He is not an uncaring God with no compassion for our weakness and struggles. There is a comfort and encouragement in this understanding. We can approach Him and know that as a father, He cares for us in all things that concern us. He abides in heaven. He exists in the realm of the Spirit. He is not an earthly king upon a temporary worldly throne. He rules in heaven. Therefore it takes faith to approach Him, for by faith we see and understand the things which are not seen.

"Hallowed be thy name." Here Jesus tells of the proper heart attitude in approaching God. Hallowed means to make holy, to look upon with great respect. Thus by praying in our hearts "Hallowed be thy name" we are humbling ourselves and acknowledging His holiness, and we approach His throne in great respect.

"Thy kingdom come." Here a proper heart attitude is expounded upon as Jesus teaches us to have a desire for God's kingdom. We can sense an urgency in this statement; a longing for the day of His kingdom. Also, a proper perspective in prayer is gained when we acknowledge the coming of a kingdom of God quite different from that upon earth today. Our hope is in that coming kingdom, not in this world. Thus we see much in this simple statement of "thy kingdom come." Jesus tells us in this statement, "have a heart that longs for God's coming kingdom. Hope for that day and acknowledge it now by faith."

"Thy will be done in earth, as it is in heaven." Certainly, God enjoys the fulfilling of His will in heaven without hindrance as the angels joyfully seek to fulfill His desires. The "in earth" request includes us as individuals in the earth, but also goes beyond to a desire for God's will and reign to be accomplished on the entire earth. We can conclude that this request is for our individual hearts as well as a desire to see the coming of the kingdom of Jesus on the earth, as promised in Scripture. This passage prompts us to lay open our hearts to desire His will and not our own, as well as leading us to desire the coming of His kingdom. The two go hand in hand, for the more we desire His will, the more anticipation we have in looking for the return of Jesus to the earth to establish His rule and reign. The kingdom of the world loses its appeal the more we seek the will of the Father.

"Give us this day our daily bread." Jesus does not teach us to pray for a week's worth of provision, nor for a year's worth or a lifetime supply. He teaches us to pray for the needs of today. This is in keeping with His command to "take therefore no thought for the morrow: for the morrow shall take thought for the things of itself. Sufficient unto the day is the evil thereof." As we exercise our faith today, we shall find God's provision sufficient. And so shall we find tomorrow. We cannot eat tomorrow's bread today, for today we only have need of today's bread. Our focus should be on the *now* of our relationship with God.

"And forgive us our debts, as we forgive our debtors." Here we are told of the operation of forgiveness, the giving and the receiving of the same. If we expect to receive God's forgiveness, He then expects us to forgive others that may have sinned against us. Thus our hearts find a proper balance and a pleasing attitude in the sight of God.

"And lead us not into temptation, but deliver us from evil." Here we see the progression from temptation to evil. If we yield and begin to enter into temptation, the logical conclusion is evil. By seeking to stay clear of the initial temptation, we will avoid the greater pitfall which follows. By asking to be guided away from temptation, we escape the greater need of deliverance once we are entangled. By avoiding temptation, we are indeed delivered, and with fewer consequences.

"For thine is the kingdom, and the power, and the glory, forever. A-men." In these simple words, as prayed from a sincere heart, we see our smallness and acknowledge God's greatness. We cast upon Him all glory, taking none unto ourselves. We acknowledge His eternal kingdom, the only true and lasting kingdom. His is not one of many kingdoms, but rather THE KINGDOM. Also, His is the power, now and forever, even though He chooses to restrain its display until a future day. All in all, Jesus threads this instruction in prayer together revealing that a humble heart and the operation of faith are essential to a productive prayer life. Such simple words hold so much more than we can see at this time.

Lord, your disciples were wise to ask for your instruction in prayer. We likewise seek your help in preparing our hearts with the proper attitude for prayer. Increase our faith and help us to see the depths of insight in Your Word. In Jesus' name we pray.

"BECAUSE THOU HAST PUT THY TRUST IN ME."
Jeremiah 39:18

Heavenly Father, we come to You seeking the peace which abides in Your presence. We find that our own minds become an enemy of peace and a source of worry and concern whenever our hearts are invaded with unbelief or our eyes are departed from You. Whatever may touch our lives, it is certainly known by You, and we seek help in remembering to bring our concerns to You, particularly in letting them remain at Your feet. Too often, we churn over adversity (or the possibility thereof) in our minds to our own distraction from You, and find torment rather than peace. The common concerns of life have a way of consuming our thoughts. Surely this is why You have said to cast all of our cares upon You. Teach us this discipline fully, that nothing may rob us of our abiding in Your peace. It is aptly written that nothing shall separate us from the love of God. Bring this confidence into a daily reality and a fortress against any intruder, for nothing can enter to disturb our place in You unless we, through our own choosing, allow the gates to be opened. We seek Your strength and help in learning to keep the gates barred to any except You. In Jesus' name we pray.

In the commonplace of daily life we may wonder how our lives stack up in the sight of God. Our efforts and accomplishments may seem dim by comparison to others. We may ask, "Does God take notice of my life?" or "Have I contributed anything to pleasing Him?" Jesus gave a heartening example of how much God takes notice, particularly of the little things which may go unnoticed by others. In Matt. 10:42 we read of Jesus saying, "whosoever shall give to drink unto one of these little ones a cup of cold water only in the name of a disciple, verily I say unto you, he shall in no wise lose his reward." God does indeed take notice of even the smallest things and counts them worthy of reward. From the widow's mite to a cup of cold water, God looks upon the heart to reward that which pleases Him with quantity having little importance.

There are two other examples of God's thoughts on similar matters in the book of Jeremiah. The 35th chapter is the story of a family, the Rechabites, whom God had noticed. In a time of rebellion against Him, and of disobedience to God's Word, the Lord cites this family as an example of obedience to their father. Jeremiah is told to bring the family to the house of the Lord and put wine before them to drink. Jeremiah does so, but they refuse to drink saying, "we will drink no wine: for Jonadab the son of Rechab our father commanded us saying, Ye shall drink no wine, neither ye, nor your sons for ever." The Lord then speaks to Jeremiah in verse 14 saying, "The words of Jonadab the son of Rechab that he commanded his sons not to drink wine, are performed; for unto this day they drink none, but obey their father's commandment: notwithstanding I have spoken unto you, rising early and speaking; but ye hearkened not unto me." Later in verse 18 and 19 we see how God blessed and honored this family for obeying their father's command. God had taken notice of this seemingly small matter. To God, this family was worthy of reward and notice as well as being used as an example to the entire nation of Israel. We read, "because ye have obeyed the commandment of Jonadab your father, and kept all his precepts, and done according unto all that he hath commanded you: Therefore, thus saith the The Lord of hosts, the God of Israel; Jonadab the son of Rechab shall not want a man to stand before me for ever."

Another story of similar events takes place in Jeremiah chapters 38 & 39. Ebedmelech, an Ethiopian eunuch in the house of King Zedekiah, takes it upon himself to help the prophet Jeremiah when all others were seeking to kill him. When Jeremiah is put in the dungeon to die, Ebedmelech seeks the King and requests that Jeremiah be set free. Ebedmelech was taking a very unpopular position in supporting Jeremiah, but he demonstrated the strength and trust in God which enabled him to take the proper stand. When princes in the kingdom were calling for Jeremiah's death, Ebedmelech stood to request his life. As we read in Jer. 38:9, "My lord the king, these men have done evil in all that they have done to Jeremiah the prophet, whom they have cast into the dungeon; and he is like to die for hunger in the place where he is." The king then allows Ebedmelech to take Jeremiah out of the dungeon. At this time, Jerusalem is under siege by Nebuchadnezzar, king of Babylon. The city is to be destroyed and the people taken captive. In the middle of this war and destruction, God speaks to Jeremiah to go to Ebedmelech and tell him, "Thus saith the Lord of hosts, the God of Israel; behold I will bring my words upon this city for evil, and not for good; and they shall be accomplished in that day before thee. But I will surely deliver thee, and thou shalt not fall by the sword, but thy life shall be for a prey unto thee: because thou hast put thy trust in me, saith the Lord" (Jer. 39:16-18).

How encouraging to note that indeed God does see the little things that go on behind the scenes and rewards accordingly. He rewards consistent obedience to Him in the common places of our lives just as surely as He noticed the family of Jonadab and the actions of Ebedmelech.

8

"LIFT UP NOW THINE EYES"
Genesis 13:14

Heavenly Father, Your ways are often not clear to us for our eyes are not always keen in the Spirit. For what we lack in understanding, please grant us an extra measure of faith and trust in You. Forgive us for the errors of our ignorance and grant unto us a clearer knowledge of Yourself. Accept as evidence of our sincerity the fact that we come to You. We come to You in the reading of Your Word, and we come to You in prayer and worship. We come for there is no one else for us to approach. There are no answers outside of You. We come and offer ourselves before Your throne wanting to know You more fully. We thank You for Your patience and love and for the shed blood of Jesus, which is the ever perfect cleansing for our sins. Beneath the blood we stand, for it has purchased us the boldness to approach Your most holy throne. Wash us afresh, and continue to draw us into the fullness of Your purpose in Christ Jesus our Lord. In Jesus' name we pray.

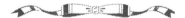

In Genesis 12 we begin to read of God's calling upon Abraham to separate himself, for God would make of his seed a great nation. Abraham then goes forth in faith not fully understanding all that would unfold before him. In verse 7, God appears to Abraham and promises that He will give to Abraham's seed this land in which Abraham is wandering. The next thing we see is that there is a famine in the land. After following God's direction and worshipfully building altars along the way, and listening to God's words of promise, Abraham finds himself in a famine. He then moves onward into Egypt for he could no longer stay in the land; the famine was so grievous. Often along the path of following Jesus we may find ourselves in a situation likened unto the famine Abraham found. We may have obeyed and in faith followed, only to find something other than what we had in mind. Never should we doubt our Lord, for He sees in an eternal perspective and the experiences we go through are necessary for God to accomplish what He wishes in our hearts.

As we read on we find that during the famine, while in Egypt, God caused Abraham to be treated very well. "And he entreated Abram well...and he had sheep, and oxen, and he asses, and menservants, and maidservants and she asses and camels." When Abraham left Egypt, we read in 13:2, "And Abram was very rich in cattle, in silver, and in gold." We can take encouragement from this event, for it is assured that we will come forth from every "famine" situation with spiritual riches of greater faith, greater trust in God, and a closer relationship with Him as we keep our eyes upon Him in each situation. The place we find ourselves may seem desolate, but as we seek the Lord in His Word, He will reveal more of Himself to us, bringing forth springs of living water in the midst of desolation.

We see that God had so blessed Abraham and his nephew Lot, that the land was not large enough to hold both of them. As we see in 13:6-7, "And the land was not able to bear them, that they might dwell together: for their substance was great, so that they could not dwell together. And there was strife between the herdmen of Abram's cattle and the herdmen of Lot's cattle." At this point we are shown a wonderful lesson in the heart and mind of God, as well as insight to the heart of Abraham. Abraham approaches Lot, his nephew, and says, "Let there be no strife I pray thee, between me and thee, and between my herdmen and thy herdmen; for we be brethren. Is not the whole land before thee? Separate thyself, I pray thee, from me: if thou wilt take the left hand, then I will go to the right; or if thou depart to the right hand, then I will go to the left." Abraham, the elder as well as Lot's uncle, was giving his nephew the choice of the land. Here we see the man to whom God had made the promise of the entire area, being totally open and releasing control into the hands of God. Abraham thought, "Take what you will Lot, I will take what God leaves me." Abraham did not say, "God has promised this to me, so I will take the best for myself." This is an admirable quality in the heart of Abraham. (Lord grant that we might seek such a heart attitude, and see what God would do for us.)

We then read of Lot lifting up his eyes and looking over the land. He notices that the plain of Jordon, over toward Sodom and Gomorah, is well watered "even as the garden of the Lord." So he chooses what looks the best to his natural eye. His spiritual eyes were closed, for we go on to read of how wicked were the cities of Sodom and Gomorah. We find later in Genesis that Lot loses everything during the destruction of Sodom and Gomorah, where he eventually lived. Often the best appearing choice is not the best choice for us spiritually. On the other hand, even famine, poverty and adversity may yield the greatest of blessings to the one whose heart is right with the Lord. In Genesis 13:14-17 we read the beautiful response of God to Abraham after Lot had made his choice. "Lift up now thine eyes, and look from the place where thou art northward, and southward, and eastward, and westward: for all the land which thou seest, to thee will I give it, and to thy seed for ever. And I will make thy seed as the dust of the earth." God had watched as Abraham allowed Lot to lift his eyes and choose. Then God turns to Abraham and says "now you lift up your eyes." The Lord rejoices to bless those whom He has chosen and those whose hearts are right before Him. We are better off to let God direct our path than to use our own human opinion outside of Him as Lot did. Though one may choose this world's best, it cannot compare to the spiritual joys of walking with Jesus. Praise God!

9

TODAY'S RIGHTEOUSNESS...
TOMORROW'S REWARD
Gal. 6:9

Heavenly Father, Your ways are past finding out. Through all things You guide and direct for our good, though we may not understand the sequence of events. Truly You come to the aid of those who put their faith in You though we be laden with infirmities and imperfections. How marvelous it is to consider Your keen interest in our lives, an interest we have done nothing to generate and can do little to maintain. It is Your nature to be concerned and loving toward Your creation. We are the recipients of great grace from You, and as we realize the magnitude of Your love, and effort on our behalf, we bow before You and express our gratefulness. Thank You Lord. You have done more for us than we could ask or think. In Jesus' name we pray.

The book of Esther is a marvelous picture of God using man to accomplish His purpose while blessing man for obedience. We see God using those who did not believe and piecing together events of the past to direct future events. There are many high points to the story upon which we will focus.

The scene was the kingdom of Ahasuerus into which the Jews had previously been carried away as captives. Through a series of events, the king decided to take a new queen, and a search was made of all the fair women of the land. Esther, Mordecai's niece, was one of the young women considered. Mordecai and Esther were Jews living in this foreign land, and we watch as God was yet very involved in their lives as events unfolded. A New Testament passage which relates this concept is I Cor. 7:18-24. It concludes by saying, "Let every man, wherein he is called, therein abide with God." As out of place as we may feel in this world, it is encouraging to see God's interest and involvement in the lives of His people who indeed were in a foreign land and out of place.

Esther was finally chosen to be queen, and the king now had a Jewish queen, although she had been instructed of Mordecai to not reveal this to anyone. While this was going on, Mordecai overheard a plot to kill the king. He faithfully reported the matter, and the plot was uncovered and prevented. A record of the event was written mentioning Mordecai as the person who revealed the evil plot. It is interesting to note that we see a captive Jew working for the good of his captor king. We see God opening doors in the earthly kingdom of Ahasuerus for His children, to later be beneficial to His people. Mordecai and Esther were living their lives, mindful of God yet unable to see the master plan at the time each step was taken.

After this event, the king promoted an evil-hearted man named Haman. Everyone bowed before Haman except Mordecai. This greatly angered Haman and he sought the king's permission to destroy, not Mordecai alone, but all of the Jews in all of the land. The king granted his request. When everything looked good with Esther as queen, a tremendous testing had come to Mordecai and Esther. God had not left them, nor had He placed them where they would be humiliated or ruined as it appeared. He had placed them where they were, for a specific reason soon to be revealed. Mordecai then sent word to Esther to petition the king for her people, saying, "For if thou altogether holdest thy peace at this time, then shall there enlargement and deliverance arise to the Jews from another place…and who knoweth whether thou art come to the kingdom for such a time as this?" (Esther 4:14) The events had unfolded, the people were in position, and yet Mordecai with faith believed, that even if Esther were too fearful to speak, deliverance would yet arise to the Jews. Esther then asked for prayer and fasting of the people for three days before she made her request to the king. Ester acknowledged, "So will I go in unto the king, which is not according to the law: and if I perish, I perish." There is no guarantee that those in the right place at the right time will fulfill God's plan, but what a tragedy if they miss the opportunity to participate in what He is doing!

Esther then prepared to request deliverance for her people, but prior to the final day when she was to ask, God moved to prepare the way for her. This is a strong indication that the prayers and fastings of the people were certainly being heard and acted upon. The night before her request of the king, the king could not sleep and asked to have the records of the kingdom read to him. During the reading, the story of Mordecai uncovering the plot to kill the king was read. The king decided to honor Mordecai, the man whom Haman was anxious to kill. Of all the records which could have been read, God caused this record of Mordecai to come before the king. How beautiful to see how righteous acts quietly build for godly results in the future. So it is with much of our daily labor. How marvelous it is to behold God working behind the scenes. He answers the prayers of His people while they yet can see nothing.

43

The king was sleepless and requested the records. Because of Mordecai's past proper actions, we see God using this in a great way. We should never lose heart in well doing as we read in Gal. 6:9, "and let us not be weary in well doing: for in due season we shall reap if we faint not." Mordecai could have justified an attitude of "why should I help the king who holds us as captive" and not done the proper thing. How much better that he did do right regardless of his circumstances. In this story, God's words of "we shall reap" are profound, for not only does Mordecai benefit, but all of the Jews in the kingdom as well (Gal. 6:9). This is certainly a clear incentive to keep a proper heart attitude in all that we would do.

In the balance of the story, we see rapid answer to prayer with Haman being destroyed, the Jews delivered and Mordecai advanced in the kingdom to the benefit of all the Jews. The story is brimming with truth for our lives today. Today's righteous acts will set the foundation for future fulfillment of God's purposes. God does hear and answer prayer, moving often invisibly to the petitioner yet never deaf to His children's cries. God holds all men and nations in His hands and directs the course of events in mysterious ways. Those who step forward in His name in the time and power of His Spirit will surely be blessed.

10

"THERE IS THEREFORE NOW NO CONDEMNATION…"
Rom. 8:1

Heavenly Father, Your Word is deep with meaning and wisdom, and yet for all our learning we merely scratch the surface of understanding the riches of knowing You. We concur with Paul's words, "for now we see through a glass, darkly, but then face to face: now I know in part; but then shall I know even as also I am known." We are quick to misunderstand and misjudge. For this we seek Your help. We measure with a partial understanding and thus build incorrect conclusions about our own life and the lives of others. Free us from these faults we pray, and let trust and faith in You be what is built within our hearts, as we leave with You the things we do not perfectly understand. You are working within the framework of eternity, while our inclination is to reason and conclude within the framework of our small experiences. Share with us Your perspective as we bring our hearts to You. We praise You and thank You for Your love and the ever present Holy Spirit who is our teacher. Help us to be good students with an ear to hear the things of the Spirit. In Jesus' name we pray.

Before we can come to know God, we must acknowledge that we are sinners and ask His forgiveness, believing in the cleansing power of Jesus' blood and His resurrection from the dead. To truly be sorry for our sins means that we must see ourselves as inadequate and unworthy to approach God of ourselves, and therefore we see the error of our own way. We acknowledge that we are not perfect, we are not righteous, and that we are in need of help. We must confess this to begin our relationship with God (I John 1:9). Seeing our sins and confessing them is necessary, but then we must also learn to accept our cleansing as complete even though we do not manifest perfection in our lives. The cleansing work of Jesus on the cross is final and perfect for all who believe. We must learn to place ourselves in that position with Christ, as being accepted by the Father, because of His sacrifice for us. It profits us nothing to labor beneath the burden of unworthiness, which we would wrongly hold upon our shoulders, when we are freed from sin through our faith in Jesus. Psalms 103:12 reads, "as far as the east is from the west, so far hath he removed our transgressions from us." We must accept this to enjoy our freedom from sin.

Romans 8:1 states, "There is therefore now no condemnation to them which are in Christ Jesus, who walk not after the flesh, but after the Spirit." This scripture states that NOW there is no condemnation. Not later when we are perfect; not later when we go to be with the Lord; not once we get everything just right and make no further mistakes, but now, today, we are not condemned if we are in the Lord. How wonderful this is to know. We may not understand why things transpire the way they do. We may struggle daily with the flesh man of sin. We may feel very inadequate. We may be assailed with the thoughts and judgments of others. We may be seeking that place of knowing God's perfect will for our lives and often feel that somewhere we missed something. But praise God that now, today, while we travel through a wide array of experiences, there is no condemnation from Him upon our lives, if we seek to dwell in His Spirit.

Our path may be through deep and dark valleys where we wonder if the sun will ever shine again. Our hearts may be wrenched with the pains and struggles of that which life deals to us, but yet we are assured that whatever our experiences in life, we are not under condemnation from the Lord if we seek His face. We may suffer the condemnation of others and be misunderstood, but this is not condemnation from above.

At times it may seem that what we feel must be God's condemnation. We look at our sin and weakness, and in ignorance we hold to that which Jesus has already taken away in the power of His love. If we look to our man of flesh and sin and admit the need for cleansing but do not turn to Jesus to receive our forgiveness, then we are choosing to stand in unnecessary guilt. Unbelief clouds our view of God's promises.

It takes an effort to walk "after the Spirit." It takes a willful effort of worship, prayer and praise to scatter the clouds of darkness that would seek to cover the Christian with condemnation. Romans 8:6 says that life and peace are for those who are spiritually minded. Peace is life without condemnation and without the burden of guilt for sin. Having once received the Lord as Savior, this place of living is for those who would continue in a life of prayer and praise. It is impossible to feel condemned when one is praising God. In true worship one is lifted above the thoughts of self and sin into the glorious acceptance of the Father. It is in this position in Christ that freedom from sin is a reality and prayer can be offered, in faith believing. In worship we understand how much He has done for us. In worship we see that He will answer our prayers. In worship there is no power that can destroy us, condemn us, or keep us from

47

that wondrous relationship with God. In worship we are empowered to face the challenges of our days with victory; without worship we are lucky to survive them. Without prayer and worship it is very difficult to walk after the Spirit. In the words of a song we see the benefits of worship:

> When my heart is...heavy laden
> and I can't seem to carry on.
> When I can't see...the way that clearly
> and my hope is nearly gone.
> (Chorus)
> In my hour of...utter darkness
> when the light of hope is gone
> When the answers...just escape me
> and I feel so all alone.
> (Chorus)
> In the power...of Thy presence
> when my soul is praising You.
> Then the darkness...has no power
> as Thy light comes blazing through.

CHORUS: To Thee...to praise...
Thy name I come! (twice)
I Lift my hands
I lift my song
To Thee...Lord...To Thee

11

"WHO ART THOU, LORD"
Acts 9:5

Heavenly Father, we come to You having yet so much to learn and having only begun to grow in Your grace. Our understanding is not perfect and our sins and errors You see far more clearly than we do. Thank You for Your great patience with us and for Your faithfulness towards us always in spite of our imperfection. We thank You for the faith to stand upon Your Word. A faith which You honor, not because of our good works, but because we believe in Your great work upon the cross. With that as our foundation, we come boldly to seek Your touch for all who suffer and are in need. Pour Your Spirit out upon the lost, the sick and the bound. Grant that our requests which we bring to You would be fulfilled to the glory of the name in which we pray...Jesus. Thank you for answered prayer, in Jesus' name.

The story of Paul's conversion is rich with spiritual lessons that are helpful to each of us in our walk with Jesus. As we ponder the life of Paul, we learn that he took God seriously and endeavored to do that which he thought was correct. In Acts 22:3 we read, "I am verily a man which am a Jew, born in Tarsus, a city in Cilicia, yet brought up in this city at the feet of Gamaliel, and taught according to the perfect manner of the law of the fathers, and was zealous toward God, as ye all are this day." Paul had knowledge about God prior to "knowing" God, and yet for all of his knowledge his response to Jesus in Acts 9 was, "who art thou, Lord?" Paul didn't know the person of God about whom he had received knowledge. The question then is, how can we learn to know the person of God through the knowledge we are able to glean from His Word?

Part of the answer is to understand the purpose of knowledge. Why do we read and study? Why do we listen to teaching about God? If our answer is to gain knowledge only, then we miss the purpose of God in giving us knowledge. Paul says very clearly in Philippians 3:10 that the purpose of learning is, "that I may know Him and the power of His resurrection, and the fellowship of His sufferings, being made conformable unto His death." To know Him is one of the purposes of gaining knowledge. A second desired result of learning is stated in Ephesians 4:13, "Till we all come in the unity of the faith, and of the knowledge of the Son of God, unto a perfect man, unto the measure of the stature of the fullness of Christ." To be transformed into His likeness is then a second purpose of learning.

Before either one of these two desired results can become a reality to some degree in our lives, the yielding of our wills from the heart must accompany knowledge. Knowledge, without yielding and the proper heart attitude, produces only inflated religious egos and self-righteousness. Paul said, after listing all of the qualifications he had as a Jew, "Yea doubtless, and I count all things but loss for the excellency of the knowledge of Christ Jesus my Lord: for whom I have suffered the loss of all things, and do count them but dung, that I may win Christ, and be found in him, not having mine own righteousness, which is of the law" (Phil. 3:8-9).

Paul had knowledge, and then he met Jesus. The next

thing that happened was an inner yielding of the heart which allowed God to illuminate the knowledge Paul had received. We read in Acts 9:6, "And he (Paul) trembling and astonished said, Lord, what wilt thou have me to do." From that moment Paul was heading down the right path. Submission was joined with knowledge and the results are very clear when we see how God used Paul.

Knowledge of God could be likened to the coffee grinds waiting for the water to be poured over them to produce the coffee. Yielding the heart to God causes Him to pour His Spirit over the things we learn and the results are "rivers of living water" flowing out of the believer's innermost being. Without yielding we have only the letter of the Word. Yielding produces the living Spirit of the Word manifest in the life of the believer. We can hear the Word and see and read it, but if we don't yield to Him it will profit us very little. We read in Acts 28 that it takes hearing, seeing, as well as understanding with the heart, before our lives are converted into something pleasing to God; "lest they should see with their eyes, and hear with their ears, and understand with their heart, and should be converted, and I should heal them." It is possible to hear and see without yielding the heart, but it is impossible to be converted without yielding the heart. A transformed life is only possible when we yield the will to God.

Knowing Him will sustain us when our understanding may fail us. We may not understand why a loved one must suffer, but knowing Jesus will put us where He will carry us through. We may not understand why it appears that God doesn't answer our prayers, but knowing Him will comfort our hearts in the times of waiting. We may not understand how the power of God is manifest, but knowing Him will give us the boldness to call upon His name for healing and deliverance, and will loosen our faith to believe God for the needs of another to be met. We may not know why adversity strikes when undeserved, but knowing Him gives us the strength to yet praise Him regardless of what we may face. When we are tried and tested, may God grant us the grace to not forget that part of the process of knowing Him is as Paul said, "that I may know...the fellowship of His sufferings, being made conformable to His death." Surely this is part of the inner work of the cross that makes more room for Him within us.

If we do not make room for Him in our hearts by yielding self will to Him, then the life-giving power of knowledge and the transforming power of knowledge is not unlocked. Colossians 2:3 tells us that all of the treasures of wisdom and knowledge are hidden in God, therefore it is God we must make room for in our hearts before the treasures begin to be unlocked. There are no short cuts to gaining the living knowledge of our Lord. Spiritual understanding comes to us a little bit at a time as we surrender a little more of ourselves to Jesus.

12

"AND THERE CAME A LION, AND A BEAR"
I Sam. 17:34

Heavenly Father, many are the challenges that daily face Your children. At times our hearts are overwhelmed by the appearance of what has come against us. Oh Lord, help us to keep our eyes upon You alone for we desperately need Your strength and comfort. Let us not be deceived by the appearance of any situation, for You are greater than any enemy that would assail us. Help us to learn from each day and each challenge that Your unfailing love and abiding presence are forever near, as You have promised. Particularly comfort those whose hearts are breaking due to the multitude of distresses that have touched their lives. Pour out of Your Spirit upon all who earnestly seek You, and in the midst of trouble reveal Yourself to the hearts of those who so need to see. Praise You and thank You for Your comfort and love. In Jesus' name we pray.

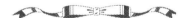

It is certainly a part of God's plan that we be tested and tried as He works to develop us into the image of His Son. The Scripture refers to "fiery trials" which denotes something more than a minor experience. Yet we do not always look upon our challenges in the light of Scripture, particularly in the heat of the turmoil. Much can be learned from the story of David in I Samuel 17 concerning the victorious life we are promised in Christ. We must remember that God never allows anything to destroy us, but rather desires us to rise in victory above each and every adversity. Even as David said, "Many are the afflictions of the righteous: but the Lord delivereth him out of them all" (Psalm 34:19).

As David kept his father's sheep, a lion came and sought to kill one of the lambs. Also, a bear had come and attempted the same. These were no little challenges when given the setting: alone in the fields with no protection, and predatory animals seeking to kill. David's response to the challenge was courageous. He did not avoid the challenge but rather went after the lion and the bear. He did not fear that which had come to destroy. He faced it with determination and trust in God. We read, "And I went out after him, and smote him, and delivered it out of his mouth: and when he arose against me, I caught him by his beard, and smote him, and slew him. Thy servant slew both the lion and the bear."

Upon these past victories, David built courage to face a bigger challenge, one for which God had been preparing him…Goliath and the armies of the Philistines. David knew that God had helped him with the lion and the bear, and as he saw the enemy defying the army of Israel he boldly proclaimed, "the Lord that delivered me out of the paw of the lion, and out of the paw of the bear, he will deliver me out of the hand of this Philistine." Had there been no lion and no bear in David's past, there would have been no foundation for the greater challenge and purpose of God. At times we may question the "lion" and the "bear" in our lives as we face certain adversities and challenges, but thank God for Scriptural examples that give us understanding as to the ways of God. Regardless of the situation, God always has our best at heart and uses all things to do His work in our hearts. As we confidently hold this to be true, we can face any adversity or challenge with courage.

The appearance of the lion and the bear were life threatening. David did not ask for these challenges, but they touched his life. David looked past the appearance and fearfulness of the situations to trust in God concerning his "lion and bear" experience. The next challenge which David faced looked much worse. Goliath was a giant of such great stature, that not one of the warriors in the entire army of Israel would accept his challenge to battle. Behind Goliath stood the massive army of the Philistines. As David looked upon Goliath, and the opposing army, he did not see an undefeatable foe, but rather saw God's ability to bring victory in the face of such odds. David's trust was not in his own skill or ability as a warrior. He even refused to wear the protective armor that Saul had offered him. He was not going to face Goliath defensively with protective armor, he was going to face him with the victory already sure because of his trust in the living God. David's armor was his faith in God.

As David went to meet Goliath, the giant proclaimed, "Come to me, and I will give thy flesh unto the fowls of the air, and to the beasts of the field." Often our challenges shout similar taunting words at our hearts: "this will destroy you" or "you can't get out of this situation" or "you are hopelessly defeated." David responded from a platform of trust and unshakable faith in God saying, "Thou comest to me with a sword, and with a spear, and with a shield: but I come to thee in the name of the Lord of hosts, the God of the armies of Israel, whom thou hast defied. This day will the Lord deliver thee into mine hand; and I will smite thee, and take thine head from thee; and I will give the carcasses of the host of the Philistines this day unto the fowls of the air, and to the wild beasts of the earth; that all the earth may know that there is a God in Israel. And all this assembly shall know that the Lord saveth not with sword and spear: for the battle is the Lord's and he will give you into our hands."

We may feel that we do not have the proper sword or spear to be victorious over the particular challenge we face, but praise God our victory is not based upon our abilities or skills but upon our faith in Jesus. From a platform of faith we can face any adversity, sickness, disease, trial or challenge and proclaim "you may have come to destroy me, and you may appear to have that ability, but I face you with courage in my faith in God and in His name you have no power to destroy me and my victory is assured in Him." We can embrace and engage any challenge knowing we shall be triumphant in our God, in His victory and power.

David ran forward to Goliath with a sling and a few small stones, and a great faith in God. God guided the stone into the giant's skull and the victory was David's. God will guide our faith to victory if we will pick it up and charge forward. Let us find encouragement from this example given us in Scripture and put to use the power of faith to embrace our challenges with expectant victory in our Lord.

13

"AND THE PEACE OF GOD...SHALL KEEP YOUR HEARTS AND MINDS..."
Phil. 4:7

Dearest Heavenly Father, there is so much we need to learn about walking in Your peace in step with Your Spirit. We are anxious about far too many things. We take into our own hands that which is to be left in Yours. Our vision is blurred by the rush of the world around us. Help us to find that place of quiet, in Your presence, that we might be refreshed and focused upon You alone. May we learn that our answers come when we are still before You, having quieted our minds so that we might hear You. Keep us in Your peace that our thoughts and actions will be breathed upon by Your Spirit and not the turmoil of all that is outside of You. Praise You and thank You for Your instruction and comfort given us through the Holy Spirit. In Jesus' name we pray.

Jesus said that He left us His peace. Many of the New Testament letters begin with a greeting inclusive of peace. The term stimulates visions of quiet pools and gentle streams that quiet the soul and refresh the spirit. Yet in this world, a place of peace seems forever elusive. Thoughts and fears and concerns pertaining to life's daily challenges seek to flood our minds and bring turmoil to the soul. Keeping pace with the basic responsibilities of life seems to chip away at any comfort of peace we may have found in a quiet moment with God. We can feel very unprotected from the harshness of the world around us and vulnerable to forces we do not want to influence us. We want peace of mind and a quiet joyful heart. Yet the flood gates of torment and turmoil can seem to be opened upon us, we find ourselves swept up in anxiety and concern, and peace has once again escaped our grasp. What is the secret to this peace of which Jesus speaks?

"And the peace of God, which passeth all understanding shall keep your hearts and minds through Christ Jesus" (Phil. 4:7). We are told here that God's peace will keep our hearts and minds. It is worthy to note that this includes both the heart and the mind. There is a connection! A heart at peace is impossible without a peaceful mind. The mind is the target for turmoil and torment born of the enemy to rob the child of God of His peace. If the mind entertains thoughts of fear and doubt sown from the enemy, then the heart is in turmoil as a result. Sometimes, it is as though we enter a whirlwind of doubt and uncertainty, and peace has fled. We can be assured that the evil one is attempting to move us from resting in God. We must exercise caution in the midst of such a storm, so that our actions and decisions are not prompted by outside forces contrary to the moving of God. When the dust of the storm subsides…in the quiet that follows…we shall know the voice of God and His peace. (It is no wonder that the Scripture speaks of girding up the loins of our minds and of the need for a helmet. I Peter 1:13; Ephesians 6:17)

One might ask, "If the peace of God is supposed to keep my heart and mind, why is it that He can't seem to keep mine?" The problem is not that He can't keep us in His peace, but rather that we keep allowing things to come between us and His peace. We must learn to reject those thoughts that are "fiery darts of the wicked" or whirlwinds of confusion from Satan, and seek the shelter of God's peace. Philipians 4:6 reads, "Be careful for nothing; but in every thing by prayer and supplication with thanksgiving let your requests be made known unto God." In other words, "Don't be worried or dwell upon the concerns that may touch your life, not even one of them. Talk to Me, your Lord, about every one of them. Let thanksgiving fill your heart, for you know I hear you and care about every detail of your life."

In His peace things become clear; problems shrink and guidance and wisdom are ever present. Peace is a very powerful thing, for the one who dwells in God's peace becomes a vessel which can be used of the Spirit. It is no wonder that the evil one seeks to remove us from that place of peace in God, for our effectiveness in God's plan is greatly reduced when we cease to be kept by His peace.

When wrestling with the torment which robs of peace, praise and worship are sure to restore us to that quiet place in God. In worship there is no place for other thoughts. The powers of darkness are scattered by the light and power of God's presence.

14

THE CONSEQUENCES OF SIN
Jer. 29:10-11

Heavenly Father, we are easily confused and dismayed by certain things which come into our lives. We do not always correctly interpret the intentions of that which You allow. Help us to see that You only have thoughts of good toward Your children. Never, even when we go astray, do You desire anything but the best for us. We may need to go through unpleasant and difficult times as a result of our own error, or because You see it is necessary for our growth, but even then Your desires toward us are that of love and goodness. As a father chastens his children, so You chasten and correct those You love. Thank You for Your faithful involvement in our lives. May we never allow circumstances to cause us to question Your love for us. In Jesus' name we pray.

Certain actions (or failure to act) will result in a consequence of that action. This is true in the natural realm of life and in the realm of the Spirit. If we are caught stealing, then we are likely to experience the consequence of some punishment. If we are found faithful and ambitious in the world of employment, then we are likely to be promoted or find success. In the realm of the Spirit, if we yield and obey God's Word, giving the Holy Spirit control of our life, we are postured to experience God's blessing. If we sin against God (whether known to others or not), then we are likely to experience a consequence of such disobedience.

Scripture shows us many examples of the consequences of sin, and more importantly, how God looks upon us during the consequence experience. There is often a stigma attached to us during the consequence by other people. This is quite distant from God's feelings toward us. When King David committed adultery and planned the murder of the woman's husband (II Sam. 11), God sent Nathan, the prophet, to confront David with his sin. David immediately confessed his sin and was informed that God had also put his sin away (II Sam. 12:13). God had forgiven David of adultery and murder. (Such an undeserved and complete forgiveness of these sins should not strike us as amazing. Jesus demonstrated this love of God toward us when He gave His life on the cross to redeem man from sin.) However, there were consequences from the sin that God did not remove! The child of the adulterous act died. David fled from the throne, from his own son, and suffered the grief of both these experiences. Important to note is the fact that once the sin was confessed and God had forgiven David, David remained in fellowship and communion with God EVEN DURING THE CONSEQUENCES. In II Sam. 12:15-20 we read that David fasted and prayed for the child. After the child's death, David worshiped. When David fled from his son Absalom, we read that upon reaching the top of the mountain on his way out of the city, David worshiped God and prayed (II Sam. 15:31-32). Later in II Sam. 17 we see this prayer was answered. The beauty of this truth is that we do not lose fellowship with God because of what we may go through as a result of the consequence of sin or ignorance. We only lose fellowship with God through sin and rebellion which is not confessed by us and forgiven by God. While David suffered a great deal of grief in his own heart, and the abusive treatment of some that observed the consequences of his sin coming to pass (II Sam. 16:5-8), he never lost fellowship with the Lord. He had confessed his sin and was truly sorry for his mistake.

In Jeremiah we read of the captivity of Israel under the hand of King Nebuchadnezzar, king of Babylon. During this time of bondage, Israel experienced the consequence of turning away from the Lord. The Lord said, that because of their rebellion and disobedience, they would experience seventy years of captivity. This was not pleasant. They were driven from their homes and their land into a foreign nation as captives. Yet in the midst of this experience, the Lord revealed His feelings toward them through Jeremiah. Jer. 29:10-11 says, "After seventy years be accomplished at Babylon I will visit you, and perform my good word toward you, in causing you to return to this place. For I know the thoughts that I think toward you, saith the Lord, THOUGHTS OF PEACE, AND NOT OF EVIL, to give you an expected end." God's thoughts and heart motives are always good toward His children, regardless of what experience we must endure on the pathway of learning His ways.

Following King David's rule, his son Solomon reigned over Israel. During his leadership, Solomon turned away from the Lord significantly. As a result, so did the people. God proclaimed that as a consequence for this sin, He would take most of the kingdom from David's family and give the leadership to another. (Splitting the kingdom into two.) In I Kings chapter 11 God chose Jeroboam as the ruler of Israel and promised to make his kingdom and leadership sure, if Jeroboam walked in God's ways (verses 37-38). Once made king, Jeroboam did not find it in his heart to trust in God's good intentions for him and his kingdom. He became fearful that if the people still went to Jerusalem to God's temple to worship, they would return to King Rehoboam (David's descendant) who still ruled over that portion of the original kingdom(I Kings 12:27). Many terrible future consequences could have been avoided if only Jeroboam would have trusted in God's Word and believed God's good intentions toward him and the people of Israel. Had he known God and trusted in Him he would have prayed, "Lord, You came to give me the kingdom. I did not ask for it. You decided to split Israel because of Solomon's sin as You told me. I will believe in Your protection and wisdom, Lord, and I will encourage the people of my kingdom to still go to the house of the Lord in Jerusalem to worship. My future, and the future of Your people, is in Your hands. I believe that Your intentions toward me and Israel are good, even as You have said. Give me strength to do that which is right in Your sight, even as we go through the consequence experience brought upon us by Solomon's sin." Had Jeroboam found it in his heart to pray such a prayer, God certainly would have honored his promise to establish Jeroboam's kingdom. How sad to read that Jeroboam and all of his descendants were cut off from the face of the earth, because he failed to trust in God's love and protection in the middle of God carrying out the consequences of Solomon's sin (I Kings 14:7-16).

It is clear that God desires to maintain fellowship with each of us continually, even during the consequences we go through as a result of our error. Surely, the "all things" that work together for good include the consequence experiences (Rom. 8:28). However, we are wise to avoid sin in the first place, for by doing so we avoid the often unpleasant experiences that result from sin.

Lord, help us to see that all of Your intentions and thoughts toward us are good and only good. In the course of life as we experience many different things, keep us from ever doubting Your love. May we never judge or question Your love by the circumstances through which we must navigate. Those You love, You chasten, and Your "expected end" for us is greater fellowship with You, which is for eternity! May we always quickly seek forgiveness for sin and error, that we may not for a moment be cut off from fellowship with You. May we commit to worship in times of blessing, in times of testing, and in times of consequence experiences. In Jesus' name we pray. A-men.

15

THE FULL CIRCLE OF
THE BLESSEDNESS OF GIVING
LUKE 6:38

Heavenly Father, we come to this place of prayer with hearts that are amazed at the depth of Your unconditional love. We stand awed and humbled as we realize that Your compassion and longsuffering causes Your care to reach past our unrighteousness, past our shortcomings and give to us the comforts of Your love. Your gentle wooing and constant desire to forgive are powerful forces which draw our seeking, though imperfect hearts to You. With each new glimpse of You, granted us by the enlightening of the Word and the Holy Spirit, we recognize how vast and unsearchable is our God, and how much more we have yet to learn. We worship You! We thank You! We give ourselves to You afresh, for Your love has drawn us to You. Fulfill Your eternal purpose in our lives. In Jesus' name we pray.

Jesus taught that it was more blessed to give than to receive. Paul encouraged the Christian to remember this teaching saying, "I have shewed you all things, how that so laboring ye ought to support the weak, and to remember the words of the Lord Jesus, how he said, 'It is more blessed to give than to receive'" (Acts 20:35). We are further prompted to give generously, by the words of the Lord in Luke 6:38. "Give and it shall be given unto you; good measure, pressed down, and shaken together, and running over, shall men give into your bosom. For with the same measure that ye mete withal it shall be measured to you again." The promise of blessing is certainly clear. There are however, things which can get in the way of our receiving God's blessing as a result of our giving.

Giving has many avenues of expression. There is the giving of time to the work and will of the Lord. There is the giving of our substance, our money, and our possessions unto others as guided by the Spirit. There is the giving of prayer on behalf of a needy soul. There is the giving of our service to help our fellow man with acts of kindness and caring, from the offer of a bowl of hot soup to continued care for a suffering loved one. The key to the blessedness which is spoken of is in the heart of the giver. More specifically, it is the heart attitude of the giver.

What is my inner motive for giving? Why do I give my money, my time, my talent or my service? This is where my own imperfections can cause me to stumble and fall, before I reach the blessedness promised. I do not desire to stumble, and I may not even see why my giving does not yield the fullness of joy in my heart. Often, patterns developed from childhood, and inner voids not yet filled with the character of Jesus, prevent my entering the blessed flow of giving. I may give with the desire for recognition, acknowledgement or approval from those to whom I give. This motive will rob me of God's blessing. The Word teaches that giving is to be "in secret." By this Jesus means that the mechanics of giving are a private matter between the giver and God, not the giver and the receiver. My attitude about giving should be to please Him, not to receive anything from the one to whom I may give. This is true whether I am giving service, prayer, or financial support. Jesus clearly explains that the only way the blessedness comes is when the attitude and heart motives are correct. In fact, if they are not, Jesus says there is no way I can expect to receive His blessing. "Take heed that ye do not your alms before men, to be seen of them: otherwise ye have no reward of your Father which is in heaven. Therefore when thou doest thine alms, do not sound a trumpet before thee, as the hypocrites do in the synagogues and in the streets, that they may have glory of men. Verily I say unto you, they have their reward. But when thou doest alms, let not thy left hand know what thy right hand doeth: that thine alms may be in secret: and thy Father which seeth in secret himself shall reward thee openly. And when thou prayest, thou shalt not be as the hypocrites are: for they love to pray standing in the synagogues and in the corners of the streets, that they may be seen of men. Verily I say unto you, they have their reward. But thou, when thou prayest, enter into thy closet and when thou hast shut thy door, pray to thy Father which is in secret; and thy Father which seeth in secret shall reward thee openly" (Matt. 6:1-6).

When I give with the wrong heart motive, or from flawed motives which I may not clearly see, bitterness and resentment may be the frequent results in my own heart. If I do not receive the recognition hoped for, or the response I inwardly "need," I may eventually begin to resent the receiver of my giving. In fact, I believe that God will purposely prevent the desired response to weed out the improper attitude in my heart. There were many sacrifices of old that were never accepted by the Lord, because the hearts of the givers were far from Him. (See Isaiah 1:11 and Isaiah 29:13.) The glorious working of the Holy Spirit is in those secret areas of my heart where He continues to conform me into the image of Christ. This is why He must prevent me from experiencing the fullness of joy in giving if my motive or attitude is incorrect; not to keep me from blessing, but to remove my flaws so I may experience the fullness of His richest blessing.

Another pitfall in giving is the danger of building self-righteousness and pride. I am reminded of the story of the Pharisee which prayed boastfully before the Lord about his giving, tithing and fasting, only to find that he was not justified before God. His heart was not adjusted properly by the Holy Spirit. (See Luke 18:9-14.) This problem can be avoided by following the advise of the Lord to "not let the left hand know what the right hand doeth." We are not to think upon our giving as though we were to receive a gold star or increased reward for each action. Let God keep the records, and let us keep on giving with abandon to the glory of Him Whom we serve.

The blessedness and joy of giving spoken about by the Lord must come "full circle" from His hand, or they will not come at all. We should never look to the receiver as the one who must be the giver of our reward for giving. God may or may not intend to bless in this way. We will find the richest of blessings when we are satisfied to receive from the hand of God our rewards for the privilege of giving. Paul articulated this attitude by saying, "I will very gladly spend and be spent for you; though the more abundantly I love you, the less I be loved" (II Cor. 12:15). Not only is this "proper motive giving" a blessing to the giver, it is also much more likely to bless the ones who receive and cause them to desire and draw near to God. Giving from the wrong "motive platform" tends to alienate the receiver, or even worse, may cause a relationship of bondage which is built out of obligation instead of love. If a person feels obligated to feed back to us the adulation, approval, or loyalty we improperly seek, our giving has a damaging effect. Proper giving should result primarily in thankfulness to God. (See II Cor. 9:11-13.) Holy Spirit–led giving has no strings attached. The blessings flow "full circle" back to us from the Lord and are in no way limited or dependent upon the response of the one who receives our gift.

In summary, although the rewards are promised, may we seek the simplicity of pleasing the Lord in all that we do, and may His smiling face be our most sought after reward. "And whatsoever ye do, do it heartily as to the Lord, and not unto men; knowing that of the Lord ye shall receive the reward of the inheritance: for ye serve the Lord Christ" (Col. 3:23-24).

THERE IS A SECOND DEATH!
Rev. 20:14

Heavenly Father, we approach Your throne on behalf of those who have not come to know You. In the rush of daily life, it is all too easy to neglect to ponder our eternal fate. We pray that Your Spirit would draw those who have, for whatever reason, ignored Your salvation. May Your Word come to them with the power of Your anointing and pierce the veil of unbelief. May the needy turn to You in the midst of distress to find Your compassion and forgiveness. Let Your Word go forth to dispel false teachings. Guide our steps in the right way. In Jesus' name we pray.

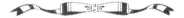

Revelations 20:14 speaks of "the second death." This raises questions concerning the first death. What is it? Where do we go after we die? Are all men treated equally after death? And then there is the question, "What is the second death?" The fact that there is a second death means that the first death (death as we know of it) is not a ceasing to exist. There are events that every one of us will experience after death. However, they are not the same for all men. At this point let me clarify that the Scripture does not support the false teaching of reincarnation, nor does it support the idea that all men go to heaven. What we are speaking about is the judgment of God on all men, which takes place after we die, and the state of our souls until that judgment.

The Scripture states in Hebrews 9:27, "It is appointed

unto men once to die, but after this the judgment." What happens until and after this judgment? Existence continues for all men! The Scripture does not tell us of any ceasing to exist, even for those of us who fall under the wrath of God. We are taught that if our names are written in the Lamb's book of life, we will live forever in heaven with Jesus (Rev.21:27). Having our name on a church roll is insufficient. Heaven is for those who have had their sins washed away with the blood of Jesus, through faith in Him. If our names are in this book, then upon death we go to be in the presence of the Lord, receiving the reward of our faith (II Cor. 5:8). The second death has no effect upon us for it does not apply to us. Thus, death for the Christian believer is a passing into the promise of life eternal in the presence of the Lord. This is a glorious event for the blood washed saints of God (Rev.20:6)!

What then is our fate if we die without having our sins forgiven through faith in the redemptive work of Jesus on the cross? The Scripture tells us that we remain quiet until one thousand years after the Lord's return to earth (Rev. 20:5). Then comes the great judgment of God when every individual will stand before Him (Rev. 20:12). After this judgment, all those whose names are not written in the book of life pass through the second death. The Bible tells us that on the other side of the second death there is existence. However, it is an existence of eternal torment. As we read in Revelations 21:87, "But the fearful and unbelieving...shall have their part in the lake which burneth with fire and brimstone: which is the second death." The Scripture makes it very clear that this second death is not a ceasing to exist as stated in Rev. 14:11, "And the smoke of their torment ascendeth up for ever and ever: and they have no rest day nor night..."

We then are given a say in the eternal state of our existence. If we reject the love of God through Jesus, we are condemned to an existence of eternal torment. To receive the love of God through faith in Jesus is to assure us of life eternal in heaven. Therefore the second death is not something that we must experience. God gives every soul a choice. While there is much more to being a Christian than assuring ourselves of a place in heaven, it is certainly the cornerstone of our faith.

How then do we assure ourselves that we can escape the second death? The answer is simple and explained clearly in John 3:16-18. "For God so loved the world, that he gave his only begotten Son, that whosoever believeth in him should not perish, but have everlasting life. For God sent not his Son into the world to condemn the world, but that the world through him might be saved. He that believeth on him is not condemned: but he that believeth not is condemned already, because he hath not believed in the name of the only begotten Son of God."

To be sure you are bound for eternal life and not eternal torment, believe that Jesus died for your sins. Believe that His shed blood and sacrificial death on the cross are the atonement and cleansing for your sins. Tell God you are truly sorry for your sins and admit that you are a sinner. Ask Jesus to come into your heart and surrender your life to Him. By His Holy Spirit, you will receive the promise of eternal life and will become what the Bible calls "born again." You will be made alive in the Spirit, quickened to eternal life through the power of the Spirit of God - the same power that raised Jesus from the dead.

The choice is yours. Don't pass up the opportunity to secure your place in heaven and avoid the torment of the

second death. Jesus loves you. He died for you. He is waiting for you to ask for His forgiveness. It doesn't matter how
sinful you have been. The blood of Jesus cleanses all sins,
great and small (I John 1:7). Ask Jesus into your heart today
while you have the opportunity, for no man knows the hour
of the Lord's return.

THE DIVINE PROCESS
Ephesians 4:15

Heavenly Father, we come to You for protection and refuge, for many are the forces which seek to deceive. Our enemy comes not looking like darkness, but rather looking like an angel of light. From such a foe we need Your divine protection. Cause us to rest in You and hear the "still small voice" of the Spirit. May the motivations of the flesh be stilled so that we hear the gentle moving of the Holy Spirit of God. Preserve us unto the day of Your coming. In Jesus' name we pray.

There is a process by which God's work is accomplished in the heart of man. This process is in harmony with God's ultimate intention for those who love Jesus, which is that we might be transformed into His image and reflect His character. This is not a small project! We were born in sin; we are self-willed; we seek our own way and have to battle with our ego. We are easily tempted to take what we learn of God and utilize it in the energies of self and soul, rather than yield them up as tools for the Holy Spirit. Perhaps we lean in this direction because we have not been taught the difference. None-the-less, the process of God working in man's heart is substantial.

We are admonished in the Scriptures to "grow up into Him in all things" (Eph. 4:15). Growing takes time. There is no instant drive-up window through which we may go to order up a completed spirituality and maturity in Christ.

Nature teaches us that growth takes time. The life stories of the great men of God also show us that growth and preparation for service take time. Let us visit just a few to see what is involved in this divine process of preparation.

Joseph, as a very young man, had a dream or a vision from God. God was revealing what He would do in the future. In Genesis 37 we read of the vision of all of Joseph's family bowing down to him, as well as many others. Joseph had this vision. It was real. But it was not for many years that it came to pass. And during those years God took Joseph through many different, and sometimes painful, experiences, all the while working in his heart. He was sold by his jealous brothers as a slave and taken to Egypt (Gen.37:28). He was falsely accused of sexual misconduct with his owner's wife and placed in prison (Gen. 39:20). Joseph lived many years in exile: raising a family in a foreign land. However, God prospered Joseph greatly until he rose to rule the entire land of Egypt, under Pharaoh. The vision was then fulfilled as God used Joseph to save Jacob's family and prosper His people (Gen.45).

Moses, as a young man, thought that his people would understand that he would help deliver them from bondage in the land of Egypt (Acts 7:25). It was forty years later, after he had fled Egypt, married, and raised children, that God spoke to him to return to Egypt to deliver His people (Acts 7:30).

David also was called. He was anointed king at a young age (I Sam. 16:13). However, his path did not lead him straight to the throne, but rather through many difficult and trying years. He served in the army under King Saul, only to be hated and pursued. He ultimately fled his home nation for fear of his life (I Sam. 18-30). Once he was made king, it was not over all of Israel, but only over Judah (II Sam. 2:4). Through many trying situations and battles, the entire nation was finally under David's rule (II Sam. 5:3).

And in remembering Joshua, he did not one day decide to lead the nation of Israel into the promised land, but was prepared as Moses' servant for 40 years in the wilderness. And even then, God had planned to give them the promised land, "by little and little" until they were increased (Exodus 23:29-30).

God's work in the heart of man takes time. There is a divine process tailored to each child of God to prepare that one for God's intention for his life. The process is the cross. The crossing out of the self-will and the learning to yield to God. The quieting of the self-motivated religious servant and the establishing of the follower of the Holy Spirit. There is a subtle counterfeit for the moving of the Holy Spirit. It comes looking and sounding good, pronouncing encouragement to act and become a doer of great things for God. The danger however, is that it is a motivational force from the soulish level and not the Spirit. It is a false voice that would say "just as Joshua decided to rise up and take the promised land, so must we" without giving appropriate reference to the many years of preparation and God's timing, which are always required for the true work of the Spirit. It is a false voice that would say, "we will take this city (or nation) for our God, in Jesus name!" While this sounds tremendously exciting and certainly appears to be of "faith," in fact it is the voice of man's self- motivation. Nowhere do we find Paul, Peter, nor even Jesus the very King of Kings making such a statement as "we shall take all of Rome for Jesus." Scripture states clearly that in the last times darkness will cover the people, and that men will turn away from God

(Isaiah 60:2; II Thes. 2:1-4; II Tim. 3;1-8). Not that Jesus will refrain from saving souls, for He will continue to save the lost, but it is soulish motivation at its peak that presumes to "take this world for Jesus." Jesus will take it when He returns!

It is easy to speak only of the great victories in Scripture, but we must also preface them by the inner work of God in the hearts, and the divine timing and planning that preceded all such wonderful works. The divine process takes us first to the cross, through the process of dying daily to self. Then wisdom, character, balanced insight and a resting in the Holy Spirit begin to grow, allowing us to follow and not grieve Him. The maturing souls of the believers do not need motivational speakers; they need Holy Spirit teachers. Motivation is a short lived boost to the mind and emotions. Holy Spirit teaching forms a foundation for continuing strength and victorious living.

We should exercise caution, lest we start work on the tenth floor of the building without proper regard for the foundations and first nine floors. Neither Moses, Joseph, David nor Joshua could have done the works of God one day prior to the Lord's appointed time. Imagine the folly of Joshua telling Moses 20 years into the wilderness (and 20 years prior to God's timing) that he had the faith and vision to lead the people into the promised land, and that it was time to go. Yet certain voices today proclaim just such a "faith." We must be careful lest we be swept up in the motivational forces of flesh and deception (veiled as faith and light). Those who move to the voice of soulish motivation will find it very difficult to hear and follow the voice of the Holy Spirit.

In conclusion, Hebrews chapter 11 speaks of the great

people of faith outlining many victories, many triumphs and answers to prayer. It concludes with "others were tortured...stoned...slain...afflicted...tormented." And it further states that "all these, having obtained a good report through faith." This is Holy Ghost faith. Faith that keeps on going when things are falling down around us! Faith that walks confidently through affliction. Faith that faces all that we may not be able to understand with the confident knowing that God is with His people. Greater than the parting of the sea...greater than the defeating of enemy armies...greater than the healing of a sick body...greater than any other thing is the precious faith of one soul. A faith which allows us to daily trust in Jesus through the midst of trials, suffering and adversity. This is the great work of God, and it is in the heart of individuals.

"BECAUSE YOUR ADVERSARY THE DEVIL...WALKETH ABOUT SEEKING WHOM HE MAY DEVOUR."
I Peter 5:8

Heavenly Father, we come to You as we have many times before, weary and in need of Your refreshing. Many are the pressures which come to burden our souls. Many are the challenges which test our faith. There is much we do not understand. Help us in all things to trust in You. Keep us with a heart to seek You that Your peace may reside within us. Protect us from the condemnation of the devil who would rob us of our joy in the midst of the testing. We claim Your protection and strength as we face that which is before us. Forgive us for our sins, and free us from the guilt associated with our errors and ignorance. We thank You for Your patience and understanding. In Jesus' name we pray.

The Christian experience is a life-long journey. It is much more than being born again, forgiven of our sins and being bound for eternal life in heaven. Along the way we will have many experiences and challenges. God desires each believer to develop in character and maturity, to be victorious over the challenges of evil, and to conquer the demands of the fallen self-centered old nature. As we read in Eph. 4:13, "till we all come...unto the measure of the stature of the fullness of Christ."

Satan is a formidable adversary. He deceives and appears as an angel of light. As we read above he is "seeking." But what is he seeking? We know that his goal is to destroy, but what does he seek to accomplish this goal, and how can we prepare ourselves to not be destroyed? God desires us to be equipped with protection against the enemy. That protection is provided through the Word of God. As our understanding is increased, and as our spiritual stature is strengthened, we are less likely to succumb to the onslaught of the devil. Without correct spiritual understanding from the Word, we are more vulnerable to defeat.

Satan seeks to destroy by working to activate and direct the flesh-man, the old nature self-centered man in each of us. This is the man that is to be "crucified with him, that the body of sin might be destroyed, that henceforth we should not serve sin" (Romans 6:6). It is essential that the believer know that yes, Satan is our adversary, but so is our flesh. If we do not recognize this enemy, we are more likely to hinder our progress in God and to aid Satan in his seeking to destroy. In Romans 8, we read of the flesh being the enemy of things spiritual "that the righteousness of the law might be fulfilled in us, who walk not after the flesh, but after the spirit…for to be carnally minded is death; but to be spiritually minded is life and peace. Because the carnal mind is enmity (in opposition and hostile) against God." Satan therefore seeks a partnership with our flesh man in order to drive us away from God's purposes. This is what he is seeking: any man of flesh who will listen to him and yield to his deceptive ways.

We must allow God to put our self-nature to death, through the inner working of the Spirit in our lives, in order to keep us safe from the enemy. In Romans 6: 11, we read sound advice to assist us in understanding how to remain free from sin and the destroyer. "Likewise reckon ye also yourselves to be dead indeed unto sin, but alive unto God through Jesus Christ our Lord…Let not sin therefore reign in your mortal body." Earlier in verses 3-7 we read of our being "dead", "crucified" and "buried with him." This is how we must reckon our self-nature in order to prevent the enemy from finding a "partner" in us to accomplish destruction.

In Romans 7, we read of the continual struggle between the old flesh man and sin, with the spiritual desire for God and the new "born again" man of the Spirit. This struggle is continuous as long as we remain in this earthly tabernacle. We must learn this and the key to overcoming.

That key is the cross, absent from much that is taught today, but necessary for true and lasting victory over the enemy. We need to learn to submit to the crossing of our wills as God puts to death the self-nature. This process hurts. It is not pleasant, but it is necessary for our own protection. Paul stated, "I die daily." The process of death to self is never over. It can never be forgotten. It is the key to our safety and spiritual maturity. We must learn to embrace the cross (the dying to self and the crossing of our wills) even as did our Lord. His final prayer was (as he was facing the ultimate dying to self) "nevertheless, not as I will, but as thou wilt." Nevertheless is a tremendous word here. Jesus is saying, "regardless of what I want, and no matter what the result is to me personally, and no matter what it may cost me, and no matter what the pain, Thy will be done Oh God, not mine." This is our example to follow. This is the heart attitude that will lead to victory and resurrection power in our lives. This is the attitude that will render the destroyer powerless.

To win over the devil, we must win over our own selfishness. If we only think to fight the devil we miss out in understanding that his target is our other enemy, our own fleshly self. We are in the battle ground with fighting waging on two fronts: the devil and the flesh. God is on our side, and the victory is sure, as long as we understand how to win. It takes the power of the Spirit to bring victory. That power is unleashed as the self is put to death and God is enthroned upon our hearts. This is not an easy message to learn. It is not as popular as other less "costly" approaches to God. Yet it is the Scriptural approach. It is the way Jesus said we should go.

Being His follower does not mean taking the easy way, for the road is uphill to the end and leads to the cross. "If any man will come after me, let him deny himself, and take up his cross, and follow me" (Matt.16:24). Taking up the cross does not mean doing only the spiritual things we enjoy. It means allowing God to take us through life to learn His lessons: maturity, responsibility, integrity, honesty and hard work. It means doing the task at hand to the glory of God, whether that task is pleasant or not, or spiritual or not in our own judgment. It means working for a living, paying our bills on time and not misusing or overextending credit financially. It means providing for a family, supporting and praying for our spouse, nurturing and encouraging our children. It means praying and worshipping day in and day out, in good times, and in trying times. It means living a life pleasing unto God in the common places of life, in private, and in public. It means living a life that is His witness, in a dark world, in the place that we find ourselves. It means trusting in God to provide for the work which He wants done. It means the death of spiritual ego. It means waiting upon God for all things and trusting in His timing. It means loving Jesus and wanting His will more than our own plans for Him or for ourselves. It means following Him, not pulling Him into our own desires.

Oh, Lord, teach us the way of the cross, and help us discern the difference between our own ambitions and Your working in us. Keep us safe from ourselves and the devil's attacks. In Jesus' name we pray. A-men.

19

"IF ANY MAN WILL DO HIS WILL, HE SHALL KNOW"
John 7:17

Heavenly Father, most holy God, we come to You and acknowledge Your majesty and power. The gifts of Your Spirit are a manifestation of Your glorious Self. They are a holy thing. They are a part of You. May we know that to be where Your gifts are operating, is to stand upon holy ground. Teach us to discern Your work and gifts from that of the impostor. May we be kept in step with Your ways and drawn closer in our relationship with You, not to be distracted by apparent spiritual things which lack Your anointing and holiness. In Jesus' name we pray.

Our relationship with God is fashioned by our understanding of Him. We need to know Him. We need to understand Him and know of His ways. This we learn through His Word. The application of truth from His Word comes to us through the Holy Spirit. The Holy Spirit applies the truth to our hearts and minds to cause us to know Him. We can trust in the application of the Word to our understanding to the degree that we embrace the cross. If we embrace the cross and yield our wills to God, then the Holy Spirit applies the Word to our understanding. To the degree that we avoid the cross and yielding our wills to God, we are open to deception and the improper application of truth. We will understand clearly to the degree that we embrace the cross.

Our love for Him is in direct response to increasing our knowledge of Him through His Word. It is impossible not to love Him as we understand Him. Only the rebellious and self-willed can profess no love for God. The yielded cry out of His great mercy and glory and tell of their adoration toward Him, for they have seen Him as He is through an understanding gained from the Word. Our worship of Him is founded properly when our understanding is based upon the truth of His Word gained by embracing the living of a crucified life.

All that surrounds the Word is peripheral and secondary in importance to gaining an understanding of God. The signs and wonders of God are not nearly as important as the Word. God will bear witness to the Word if it is correctly taught, to cause the Word to be received. Signs and wonders which do not line up with the Word, or which accompany teaching and behavior not in line with the Word, should be questioned. Where there is spiritual activity with the gifts, yet no teaching of the Word and the cross, there is at least improper emphasis, and very likely deception. The gifts cannot be taught. There can be no seminars on how to operate the gifts of the Spirit. Such talk is in itself rooted in misunderstanding. God will follow the correct teaching of the Word with the manifestation of the gifts, signs and wonders. Therefore signs and wonders are not what we are to seek after, nor what is to be taught. We are to teach the Word. We are to seek after the correct teaching of the Word and the rest will follow. When the teaching is about the death to self through the work of the cross, the power of God will be present. When one tries to teach about the power of God absent the cross, the wrong power will be present. When one tries to teach about the gifts of the Spirit, the signs and wonders of God and how to make them appear, then incorrect emphasis invites the wrong power. It is true, that we are encouraged to desire spiritual gifts. They are a beautiful and special part of the Christian experience. However, there must be the proper preparation of the heart, or we will be attempting to put new wine in old wine skins.

There is a dire need to teach the Word of God, and that there is no substitute for the cross. We need to learn there must be a yielding to God and a death to self before any godly power will be manifest. The power is not what we are to seek after. If we seek to know Him, love Him and understand His Word, He will manifest Himself. It is His Word. They are His gifts. The signs and wonders come from His hand. They are the gracious manifestation of God Himself, when He beholds the hearts that are focused upon His Word and seeking Him, not His manifestations. We get it all wrong when we seek that which is to follow the Word and not the Lord Himself. In Psalms 103:7 we read, "He made known His ways unto Moses, His acts unto the children of Israel." It is His ways that God wishes us to learn. It is a shallower experience to know only His acts. And to seek His acts of themselves is to misunderstand their purpose. They are the extra blessing, the added confirmation, but not the main ingredient. The main ingredient is the PERSON of God, and to know Him is the central message.

In Mark 16:20 we read, "And they went forth and preached everywhere, the Lord working with them, and confirming the word with signs following." They did not go forth preaching the signs, the wonders, and the gifts. They went forth teaching the Word, and the signs followed. If the signs are not following, we should examine our hearts and seek to better deliver the Word. To seek the signs is dangerously out of order. When we get it right with the Word, God will do His part to confirm the same.

20

"I HAVE YET MANY THINGS TO SAY UNTO YOU, BUT YE CANNOT BEAR THEM NOW."
John 16:12

Heavenly Father, You are unchanging in Your faithfulness. You are truly the Rock upon which our salvation stands sure. The winds of confusion may blow to and fro over the sea of mankind, yet in You there is stability and safety from the storm. Focus us upon those things which are eternal that we may build, and be built up, in the Spirit. Grant us the discernment to know the things which are of You, and let us shun that which comes from any other source. Keep us unto the day of Your coming. In Jesus' name we pray.

Jesus, in speaking as he did in John 16:12, displays the understanding of the spiritual condition and abilities of those to whom He was speaking. He who was teaching knew what could be handled by those being taught. There were things which the hearers could not "bear." They could not lift or handle certain things yet. One could envision a young child attempting to pick up and use the sword of a soldier. While His audience may have been comprised of adults, Jesus knew their stature of spiritual maturity and did not give them what they could not handle.

Paul, a great teacher gifted by the Holy Spirit, shared similar statements. In I Cor. 3:2 we read Paul saying, "I have fed you with milk, and not with meat: for hitherto ye were not able to bear it, neither yet now are ye able. For ye are yet carnal." With all of the great and exciting teachings of Jesus, there was also a frankness which let those who would hear know where they really stood. With Paul, there was also this straight forward honesty which promoted spiritual maturity. In Hebrews 5:13 Paul says, "For every one that useth milk is unskillful in the word of righteousness: for he is a babe. But strong meat belongeth to them that are of full age, even those who by reason of use have their senses exercised to discern both good and evil."

Spiritual maturity comes only one way, the way of the cross. Through the crossing of the will, God makes more of His likeness visible in the believer. Paul states in I Cor. 3:3 that some of the believers were carnal. They were babes in the Spirit. They were thinking they had attained a spiritual level which in truth they had not. They had not yet been through the inner yielding to God through the work of the Spirit. They were zealous concerning godly things, but zeal does not equate to spiritual maturity.

A look through the first book of Corinthians reveals that there were spiritual gifts operating but not orderly and not for the proper reasons. By reading chapter 13, one gets the clear impression that love was not the motive behind the gifts, as Paul spends a great deal of time speaking on this subject. In chapter 14, he admonishes all things to be done unto edifying, decently, and in order. Earlier in the book we are told it was commonly reported there was fornication among the church. There was arguing and disputing between brethren resulting in the equivalent of lawsuits (chapter 6). There was ignorance concerning participation in offerings to idols (chapter 8). As we put all of this together, we get a picture of widespread spiritual immaturity and the resulting confusion. But then we also see Paul. God had a voice to help sort out all of the mess and get things on the right track. We also see God's love and patience through Paul. We can sense Pauls' love for the Corinthians, as he endeavors to correct them and build them up. He often calls them brethren, displaying his oneness with them in their growth and learning.

Doing God's will in yielding to the work of the Spirit <u>is to let go of what we want to do for Him</u>. Starting out on the road to spiritual maturity is not to necessarily head off to a foreign mission field or give up all responsibility to "serve God full time." There is an excitement to some of these ideas that may well be quite the opposite of the crossing of our will in yielding to the cross. Seeing and believing is only the beginning. Moses knew his people needed deliverance and felt he would help them. It was 40 years later that all things were ready.

And what is yielding to the cross? It is most likely not a grand and spectacular sacrifice, but rather it is found in the everyday common places of life. It is the daily event used with mastery by the hand of God to touch us inwardly where He sees we need to change. It is the thing which humbles us in our own sight. It is the circumstance which guides us to give up some cherished plan or earthly treasure, while God watches to see how gracefully we yield it up to Him. It is the thing which reveals to us that we sought to better our own reputation rather than glorify Jesus. It is the thing which comes to put to death our pride-filled ambitions which seek the accolades of man. It is the pressure that stretches us inwardly to make more room for the "new wine" of the Spirit. It is all of the little things which add up to empty our selfishness and replace it with the character of God as described in I Cor. 13:4-7.

89

There are no short cuts to growth in the spirit. Believers can be unwittingly misled by teachings concerning the gifts of the Spirit: premature to the realization of a maturity level that would allow them to "bear" the responsibility of the gifts they seek. The laying on of hands is not a casual showing of concern. Nor is it to be carelessly encouraged. It is an ordained spiritual activity carrying the power of God and requires a preparedness to stand against the evil in the spiritual realm that would assail another. The gift of knowledge is not an inquisitive guessing game of "do you have a problem with this or that?", but rather a sacred and divine revelation given to accomplish a specific work. There is no doubt in it when it is from God. Some workers may attempt to imitate the concept of the gift, not realizing the difficulty they may bring upon the soul of another through their ignorance and error. When we see these things, are we not witnessing the same disorderly activity which Paul wrote to correct in Corinth? If the teaching emphasis is on the "strong meat" activity of maturity, there must first have been the milk of the Word. There must first have been an embracing of the crucified life. There must be a discernment from the teachers as to what others can bear, or we will find children in the Spirit seeking to use the weapons of the soldier.

21

"FOR THOUGH HE WAS CRUCIFIED THROUGH WEAKNESS"
II Cor. 13:4

Heavenly Father, as we are pressed upon by the things of this world, our vision is sometimes clouded. Darkness seeks to sow the seeds of doubt as we behold the ravages of the battle against sin and evil. We look about and do not always behold victory. But in You, our victory is sure and the struggles we behold are brief disturbances along the way. Our hope remains in Your resurrection and the promise of Your return. With eternal life as our promise, we do well to not let the days' troubles have more power than they should. When our thoughts are on You and Your kingdom, all else that may touch us is reduced to nothing. Hasten the day of Your return, for we long to greet You and enter fully into that which our hearts have tasted. Teach us the discipline of keeping our eyes upon You, for in doing this our hearts will have peace. In Jesus' name we pray.

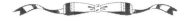

What is this "weakness" which led Jesus to the cross? How can it be said that the Son of God was weak? As we ponder this statement we see that the only weakness Jesus had was the body of flesh in which he dwelt, a body which was weak enough to suffer death like all men. As we look beneath the appearance of weakness, we behold a supernatural strength and Godly power. For it took God's power in Jesus to allow Jesus to proceed to the cross, when He continued to possess the power to NOT go to the cross.

Jesus knew that the ordained steps of His life would lead to the cross. He beheld the cross knowing what would happen to Him when He got there. With perfect obedience to God's plan, He wavered not from the path but determined to take each step necessary to fulfill dying on the cross to redeem lost man. When Peter tried to defend Jesus in the garden of Gethsemane and drew his sword, Jesus said, "Put up again thy sword into his place...Thinkest thou that I cannot now pray to my Father, and he shall presently give me more than twelve legions of angels? But how then shall the scriptures be fulfilled...?" (Matt. 26:52-54) Jesus refused to waver from the path of the cross. Inwardly, He was charged with power to complete the purpose of His coming. In Gethsemane, Jesus saw the suffering He would endure and chose to embrace it. Weakness would not have done so. Jesus didn't run to get the suffering over with, nor did He turn from the path toward it. He took each step and with determination obediently took the next. With each step He embraced the will of God and accepted the suffering and shame as the plan of salvation unfolded.

Jesus knew of the victory that was waiting for Him after the cross, for we read in Hebrews 12:2, "Who for the joy that was set before him endured the cross, despising the shame, and is set down at the right hand of the throne of God." We ourselves are given the same promise throughout Scripture, as we are promised eternal life and the forgiveness of our sins. We are told to look to Jesus as our example in the times when we may be seeking to avoid the cross as it touches our lives. We read in Hebrews 12:2-3, "Looking unto Jesus the author and finisher of our faith...For consider him that endured such contradiction of sinners against himself, lest ye be wearied and faint in your minds." We are asked to embrace the path of the cross just as Jesus was. And it is through His Spirit within that we find the power to take each step with determination and not waiver. As we yield to His will within us, our hearts will say, "I will endure the cross and not turn from it, for I see the joy and glory that lies on the other side of obedience." Jesus shared our weakness in the flesh. He knows and understands our struggles. Through His Spirit we share His power to overcome.

Regardless of the trials and troubles which touch us, we find hope in the truth that Jesus rose from the dead. If He rose from the dead, then we too shall rise from the dead, and anything that happens to us between now and then, let it be to the fulfilling of His will. For what comparison can we make with our troubles, when we place them in the perspective of rising from the dead, to spend eternity with Him, free from our sins. This is the joy set before us. Let us not take our eyes off of it. Jesus died, shed His blood to cleanse us of our sins and rose from the dead to proclaim His promise to all believers of eternal life. This should be our focus. This is our hope and promise. This is our source of joy. Why should we spend one moment in sadness of heart when the kingdom of God has been offered to us as our home forever? And why should we waiver from the path of the cross, when He has asked us to follow, and the fullness of joy is given as our reward? "And whosoever doth not bear his cross, and come after me, cannot be my disciple" (Luke: 14:27).

22

"FOR THEY KNOW HIS VOICE"
John 10:4

Heavenly Father, in this time of so many voices seeking to direct our paths, we ask You to teach us of Your voice. We ask to always be given a hunger and thirst for the things of the Spirit and to learn to always yield to Your will. Help us pay the price of obedience to the Holy Spirit's call. May those who are confused find peace and light in Your presence. We pray against the powers of darkness that seek to hinder the work of the Holy Spirit, and we ask for a mighty outpouring of Your anointing upon the work that You would do. Help each of Your children to trust more in You and see You more clearly. In Jesus' name we pray.

In the tenth chapter of John, Jesus gives us a beautiful description of Himself as the Good Shepherd. He tells of His great love for His followers, in that He is the only one who will lay down His life for the sheep. He explains that when the sheep are threatened, He will not leave them alone as a hired person would do. He tells of the joys of having Him as our shepherd, saying, "by me if any man enter in, he shall be saved and shall go in and out and find pasture." He further states His purpose of coming to be our shepherd, saying, "I am come that they might have life, and that they might have it more abundantly." He compares Himself to others by describing them as "thieves and robbers" come to "steal, kill and to destroy." Such a comparison, coupled with Jesus' description of Himself as the Good Shepherd, makes us desire Him to be our shepherd. Knowing His promises for us, it is natural that we should want to have Him guide us and watch safely over us as we walk through the pastures of life.

One of the keys to finding ourselves in His pasture is as He said, to "know his voice." The sheep Jesus describes in John 10 know his voice, and also know when the voice is NOT His. "And when he putteth forth his own sheep, he goeth before them, and the sheep follow him: for they know his voice. And a stranger will they not follow, but will flee from him: for they know not the voice of strangers." How then can we know His voice? How can we discern the difference between the many voices competing for our attention: the voice of the flesh, the voice of other people, the voice of the evil one, the voice of religious men, and the voice of the Holy Spirit? How often we can look back to past experiences and see much more clearly than looking forward. It is easy to look back upon our mistakes and see when we listened to the wrong voice. The heart's cry of the one seeking to follow Jesus is to move forward with the same clear vision. The secret is in learning to know Him and His voice; then the counterfeit will likewise be discerned.

By example in Scripture, Jesus reveals Himself to us. We know that above all else He placed the highest priority on obedience to the Father. We also know that He placed the least priority on His own will: continually dying to His own wishes and choosing to obey the Father's will at all times. To say it in the simplest way possible, we will know His voice when we yield control of our lives to Him. We will know His voice if we read His Word and spend time with Him alone in prayer and worship. The less of this we do, then the more susceptible we will be to the influences of "other voices."

Decisions to follow Jesus' voice are not always easy. There is a price of surrendering all to Him that is very real, and often reaches to the depths of our hearts. Obedience to Him does not necessarily bring peace among people. On the contrary, the more Jesus obeyed the Father, the more people were moved against Him. Jesus says in Luke 12:51-53, "Suppose ye that I am come to give peace on earth? I tell you, Nay; but rather division; for from henceforth there shall be five in one house divided, three against two, and two against three..." Such is one example of the price of obedience.

There are many sheep in the pastures around us. Many sheep follow after many different voices. We should not think it strange that at times we seem to walk alone. Jesus said, "Enter ye in at the strait gate; for wide is the gate, and broad is the way, that leadeth to destruction, and many there be which go in thereat; because strait is the gate, and narrow is the way, which leadeth unto life, and few there be that find it" (Matt 7:13-14). It should come as no surprise that many people follow the voice of man more than the voice of the Spirit. This is true because not many of us are willing to pay the price to spend sufficient time alone with God in prayer, worship, and in the study of the Word to be able to discern the voice of God. Therefore it is easier to listen to the voice of someone we presume to be telling us what God wants us to hear. To try and test the voice is not something we can do without spending time alone with Jesus.

All of the sheep belong to God. As the sheep make up their own minds as to which voice they will follow, we should not be influenced by the pathway another person chooses. Ours is to seek to know His voice and to obey Him regardless of the cost. In his letter to the Galatians, Paul marveled that the sheep had chosen to follow a stranger's voice. He spoke powerfully to help them focus again upon Jesus and the work of the Holy Spirit. In I Corinthians, Paul addressed the problem of the sheep looking to the leaders rather than to Jesus, for they were saying, "I am of Paul... I am of Apollos." Some will always listen to a stranger's voice, for they will never sit still long enough to learn of His voice. Jesus wants us to know His voice. He wants us to obey His voice. If we will, then we can perhaps be of assistance to others in reminding them to keep their eyes upon Jesus and none other. It is important to teach others not to trust in religious groups or the charisma of any given leader: but to trust in the living God and the Holy Spirit who will lead, guide, and teach each and every soul that will look to Him through Jesus.

The motives of the ones hearing Jesus' voice are to see just one other soul hearing the voice of the Good Shepherd. If we fail to teach others to hear His voice, then no amount of apparent religious success is of any value. God does not want His sheep at the mercy of many voices. As the sheep are fed by the anointing of the Holy Spirit, they will know the Spirit's voice. It is better to sit with a few and hear the voice of the Spirit than to sit with hundreds and hear the voice of strangers.

As the sheep are taught to try the spirits, fewer will follow wolves in sheep's clothing. In Matthew 7, Jesus explains that many religious ministers who appear to be serving God are not His servants. He says of them, "I never knew you." If He never knew them, then they never knew

97

His voice, and the sheep that followed these men were never taught to hear His voice. "By their fruits ye shall know them," Jesus said. When we see lives that are not right with God, regardless of their status, we should not follow; for they are not representatives of the voice of the Good Shepherd.

23

"...THE VEIL IS UPON THEIR HEART"
II Cor. 3:15

Heavenly Father, we bring to You our many concerns and heart felt pains, our tears and innermost longings. Into Your gentle and caring hands we place our most precious treasures. We have labored to preserve them and are learning that we cannot. We have wearied our souls with cares for things we cannot control. Let the time past be sufficient for not releasing all into Your care, for when we are burdened our life is a blessing to no one. Today, we give all that burdens our hearts to You. Today, we rejoice in Your love. Today, we praise You. Let our time be spent in praise, even when our perceived treasures vanish and we understand not, for You, Lord, are our only true treasure. In Jesus' name we pray.

In any area of our heart where we resist yielding to the work of the Spirit, a "veil" remains upon our heart. This is a veil that blinds us from the glory of God's fullness in that area and prevents the glory of the Lord from radiating through our lives. It is a veil that blinds our understanding. God does not want a veil between us and His revelation. He desires us to see and understand. It is our lack of yielding all things to His control that veils us from the truth and way of the Spirit. It is not always easy to yield important things over into the hands of God. We want to stay in control. We want to direct things to our own desired conclusion. We may feel that our desire is God's, but if our actions are motivated from behind the veil where an unyielding self seeks control, we are not abiding in the Spirit: And works of the flesh are the result rather than the work of the Holy Spirit. Much activity of the believer today is from behind the veil, thus we see strife, confusion and a lack of authority and power. When God gets us out from the veil, the Spirit will move and the anointing of the Spirit will flow. When the veil is removed, Jesus is the only focus. While the veil remains, our priorities are ordered in a realm not fully in the Spirit, and our energy is spent in worldly or religious ways rather than in the Spirit. The veil of the temple was torn when Jesus was on the cross (Matt. 27:51). The veil in our own hearts will also be removed, when we come to the cross and yield, from our very core, our will to Him in all things. Behind the veil, man moves in a fleshly realm attempting to accomplish spiritual things. This cannot be done, for the veil is not removed until our will is put to death by the inner work of the cross in our hearts. "But when it shall turn to the Lord, the veil shall be taken away" (II Cor. 3:16).

24

"IF IT BE POSSIBLE
LET THIS CUP PASS FROM ME."
Matt. 26:39

Heavenly Father, it is a privilege to come once again unto You. You are forever unchanging and a certain place of refuge Who never forsakes us. Your patience and understanding are more than we deserve. Over time, You make known unto us Your ways and for this we are grateful. Through every experience You bring eternal light and understanding to us as we look to You. Things which we once embraced as truth are gently removed and replaced with the greater love and light from Your Word. Each day is exciting, Lord, for in it lies the possibility of learning yet more. Make us have teachable spirits and bring us into the fullness of living in the Spirit. In Jesus' name we pray.

Jesus said to take up our cross and follow Him. To grasp a portion of the meaning of this, let us look at our Savior as He faced His cross. As He prayed in the garden of Gethsemane, knowing that very soon He would be taken and crucified, He looked at that which was terrible beyond our comprehension. The very Son of God looked at His cross and prayed to the Father, "O my Father, if it be possible, let this cup pass from me." What he beheld was foreign to His life. It would take His life. His flesh cried out for it to be removed for He did not like it. He would not have been found praying thus if he liked what was before Him. He did not like it. Then, with godly determination He added to His prayer, "nevertheless not as I will, but as thou wilt." He of Himself would have willed for it to be removed, but His inner spirit and commitment to God drove Him to yield to the Father's will. Jesus is found praying this not once, but three times before He had the matter settled. This tells us of the great consternation taking place within Him in these moments of facing the reality of the cross.

We do not always understand the work of the Spirit in our hearts. Often what God presents is foreign to our thinking. Often we do not like what we see coming or are asked to do. If we can accept the truth that the cross, and God's work in the heart, do not always feel good or comfortable, then we are postured for growth. With growth comes blessing, but before blessing comes obedience to God. When something shatters our preconceived ideas, overturns our desires, or hurts, the chances are it is good for us. We find this same principle in the parable of the corn of wheat as we read in John 12:24, "Except a corn of wheat fall into the ground and die, it abideth alone: but if it die, it bringeth forth much fruit."

Discernment is necessary to tell the difference between yielding to the work of the cross and placing religious garments upon an unyielded self. It is easier to do the latter but the results are poor. Paul, before his conversion, was full of religious activities and clothed with a marvelous religious pedigree. All the while however, he was fighting Jesus instead of yielding to Him. The Pharisees were clothed with many religious deeds and actions, so much so that Jesus called them "whited sepulchres", which appeared outward-ly wonderful but inside were full of dead men's bones.

A simple example of the difference is told us in Luke 18:10-14. "Two men went up into the temple to pray; the one a Pharisee, and the other a publican. The Pharisee stood and prayed thus with himself, "God, I thank thee, that I am not as other men are, extortioners, unjust, adulterers, or even as this publican. I fast twice in the week, I give tithes of all that I possess." And the publican, standing afar off, would not lift up so much as his eyes unto heaven, but smote upon his breast, saying, "God be merciful to me a sinner." I tell you, this man went down to his house justified rather than the other: for every one that exalteth himself shall be abased; and he that humbleth himself shall be exalted." In this story, the religious and apparent sacrificial activity of prayer, fasting, and tithing were resulting in the Pharisee exalting himself in his own eyes. This "sacrificial" activity was not the work of the cross, or the Spirit, in his heart. He took these things upon himself to clothe himself with religious activities without ever yielding the heart properly to the Lord. On the other hand, the publican came with no works to boast of, no grand sacrificial activities, and fell before God humbly asking for mercy, realizing his true state. God then takes upon Himself to clothe this publican with justification. Our works are of no value in bettering ourselves in the sight of God. It is the heart attitude that God seeks to make right.

The results of the work of God in the heart lead to a state of "being" in Him, not doing things alone. Our thinking and actions are changed from the inside as we yield to God, not clothed from the outside with religious activities. We become in our existence and expressions more like Jesus. We are more loving, more patient, more forgiving, more compassionate in all of our life, as Jesus takes us through the cross as He intends. All of the sacrifices we can possibly make are worthless without this inner changing as a result of the Spirit's work (I Cor. 13). As we abide in Him,

103

all that we do in life becomes a sweet savor unto God, from the simplest ordinary task to the precious moments of worship. Without this right heart attitude even the greatest of sacrifices is not accepted or of benefit. Psalms 51:16 &17 says it well, "For thou desirest not sacrifice; else would I give it: thou delightest not in burnt offering. The sacrifices of God are a broken spirit: a broken and a contrite heart, O God, thou wilt not despise."

We cannot make our own cross to bear. We cannot make uncalled for religious sacrifices to hasten our growth. In all that we live through, the common and the divine, we shall bear the fruit of the Spirit more fully to the benefit of all, as we learn to rest in Jesus and trust Him to accomplish His good work in our hearts. The Pharisee may have appeared to all to be far ahead of the publican, but in God's eyes his accomplishments were a hindrance. While the Pharisee may have thought himself a blessing to others, the publican was more likely used of the Spirit (though unaware to him) because of a proper heart attitude. We bear fruit because of the inner work of the Spirit, not because of our works. We should stay clear of the error which thinks that works of themselves are pleasing to God. Unless born of the Spirit of God from within, they are no more pleasing in us than they were in the Pharisee. The work of the cross is not measured by works, but by the fruits of the Spirit. "But the fruit of the Spirit is love, joy, peace, longsuffering, gentleness, goodness, faith, meekness, temperance" Gal. (5:22-23).

It is to the fruit of the Spirit that others are drawn, and thus drawn to Jesus. Sacrifices and religious works which are not born of the Spirit are as a fruitful tree painted on a wall. They may look good and be accomplished quickly, but they are of no use to the passers by. Fruit of the Spirit which is the result of the work of the cross in the heart, is like an orchard of fruitful trees bearing nourishing fruit to all who come near. It takes years for a tree to develop fruitfulness, whereas a painted wall can look good in a day. May God grant us the grace to yield to His precious work and discern the difference between our premature self-motivated actions and sacrifices, and the true work of the Spirit. Grant Lord, that Your fruitfulness may abound within us to the benefit of those around us.

25

"HE HATH NOT DEALT WITH US AFTER OUR SINS."
Psalm 103:10

Our Father and our Savior, to You we are grateful. Your love and acceptance is a free and undeserved gift. Let us not grieve You by hesitating to accept gladly that which You greatly desire us to have. May we be given grace to keep our eyes upon You, and Your love for us, in the midst of all that may touch our lives. You have known of our imperfections far before saving us. They did not stand in Your way when You first saved us. May they not hinder our relationship with You now by our focusing on them instead of You. We worship You and thank You for Your unconditional love. In Jesus' name we pray.

As we journey through this life we experience many different circumstances. Some of them we seem to understand while some leave us wondering. When good things happen to us we relate them to God's love for us and feel comforted, associating the good things with a feeling that God is pleased. When trials, testings or hardship touch our life, it is easy to feel that God is moving away from us and that the "bad" which has come is the result of our sin or error in the sight of God. Because we realize that we fall short of the perfection and righteousness of God, it is easy to accept condemnation; particularly when we do not understand the "why" of our circumstances. This is certainly not God's intention. When we accept condemnation and thoughts of uselessness, Satan has succeeded in disabling a servant of the Lord. When our eyes are upon our own failures or shortcomings, we tend to listen to Satan's condemnation and it seems to fit. We must remember that it is those very shortcomings that Jesus saw and died for. They are covered in His blood and washed away. God's love is not determined by our circumstances. His love is constant and unchanging whether we are in good or bad situations. The process of perfecting us may not be complete, but there is no condemnation to those who are in Christ Jesus.

Truth is a wonderfully freeing power. Yes, we are of ourselves worthless. Yes, we deserve condemnation. Yes, of ourselves we are useless to God. It is all true! But the greater truth is that because of all of this, Jesus shed His precious blood to wash us of our sins and make us worthy in the sight of God. This is the power of God and gift of God to all who believe in Jesus. We may fail a thousand times and stumble even more, but not one such failure changes the love God has toward us nor the power of His Word. We may seek a safe harbor from the storm of thoughts that seek to drive us from trusting in and accepting God's love, but the winds will cease and the storm become quiet the moment we place our eyes upon Jesus and once again embrace His word as true, accepting it as His gift to us.

Psalm 103 says it so beautifully, "He hath not dealt with us after our sins; nor rewarded us according to our iniquities. For as the heaven is high above the earth, so great is his mercy toward them that fear him. As far as the east is from the west, so far hath he removed our transgressions from us. Like as a father pitieth his children, so the Lord pitieth them that fear him. For he knoweth our frame; he remembereth that we are dust." These words cannot be improved upon. He has not given us what we deserve because of our sins, but rather has had mercy upon us. He has taken our sins and cast them far away. He knows our frame, our sins, our weakness and faults, and yet comes to us through Jesus to bless us and draw us unto Himself. Condemnation does not fit into the context of God's expression of love toward us.

Satan cannot rob us of our peace in God unless we allow thoughts born of darkness and lies to dwell in our hearts and minds. The mind truly is a battlefield and I Peter 1:13 states it very well, "Gird up the loins of your mind, be sober, and hope to the end for the grace that is to be brought unto you at the revelation of Jesus Christ." We are not to allow any interruption in our hope in God's promises and love toward us. We are to hold our hope in His Word until the very end. Condemnation seeks to break our "hope connection" with God and send us into a joyless, powerless, useless life. We are not to let the enemy succeed.

Our worthiness and usefulness to God is not conditioned upon religious activity, church membership, or the acceptance of man. In fact, such measurements can provide a false feeling of comfort based upon man's opinion rather than faith in God. Jesus would have found it difficult to feel worthy by relying upon the opinions of man. One day the opinion would have made Him King, and shortly thereafter it was calling for His death.

Jesus' words in John 16:12 have a good chance of applying to each of us in those things which we do not clearly understand, "I have yet many things to say unto you, but ye cannot bear them now." Let us find rest from the tormenting storm by placing in the hands of God those things which we cannot understand, and never let Satan get his hands on our trust and acceptance of Gods' love and mercy toward us. Let us remember that, "He hath not dealt with us after our sins; nor rewarded us according to our iniquities." Praise God!

26

PREDESTINED!
Romans 8:30

Father God, the depth of Your Word is amazing! As we are shown new glimpses of understanding, we realize that we only scratch the surface of the great truths of God. Even as man walks upon the surface of the earth but cannot clearly see to its core, so we walk in the shallows of all that lies beneath the sacred pages of Scripture. Take our hearts and minds and reveal more of Yourself unto us. Thank You for the Holy Spirit, which gives us deeper understanding as we yield our hearts to You. Take us as deep as we are capable of going, for it is our desire to learn more. In Jesus' name we pray.

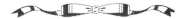

Christian living is not a haphazard experience. If I have no purpose in my life, then I dwell in a terrible state of existence. When I have a goal or objective to accomplish, then value and meaning are added to my life. God is a God of purpose. He does not gamble with my destiny. He wants me to understand His purpose for my life. I face the challenge of trying to figure out His plan for my life. God will not keep it a secret from me if I take the time to look. He is merciful and gracious and stands anxious to help.

I must expand the horizons of my thinking to begin to grasp God's plan. Being human and living on this planet we call earth, I tend to relate everything to my earthly experience. I want to know what God's plan is for "my life," as I call it. "My life" being the days I have to live on earth. This is at least what occupies much of my contemplation. God however, is thinking in terms of eternity. For me to grasp His intentions, I too must begin to think in terms of eternity. As I lift my eyes past the earthly experience and into the ages beyond, then, and only then, do I set my mind in the proper state to grasp some of God's wonderful intentions. Too often, I tend to think of this life as the "after graduation" experience. As a student anxiously awaits graduation from school to begin his "own life," so I look for that day on earth when I will step into my "purpose." God is looking far past my purpose in this life to fulfill His purpose for me as it relates to eternity.

What is His purpose? What has He planned? A good place to start looking is where Scripture speaks of being "predestined." These are the things that God has predetermined, or planned for us in advance. These are His interests in accomplishing His purpose for me and for you. Somewhere, before time began, God set out a goal for me and you. He planned that we would come to this ultimate purpose as the ages unfolded. He then set the machinery in motion to bring us to that predetermined goal. "For whom he did foreknow, he also did predestinate to be conformed to the image of his Son" (Rom. 8:30). God plans for each of us to be made into the image of Jesus. This is a personal, individual goal for each believer. This intention of God reaches beyond what we may accomplish or not accomplish in this world. This purpose of God is the making of godly men and women. It is the building of integrity, compassion and strength of character. The school we are enrolled in is called "planet earth." Every moment of every day has a purpose in God bringing me and you to the day of graduation; that day when the body shall rest and return to the earth, and our eternal soul will rise to be with the Lord forever.

God's eternal purpose is different from any ministry or work we may be given to do while in this "school." God tells us in Ephesians 2:10, "For we are his workmanship, created in Christ Jesus unto good works, which God hath before ordained that we should walk in them." As part of our schooling, we are to walk in "good works" that are preordained by God. This, however, is not God's eternal purpose. This is His "earthly purpose" for us. The works of ministry, of giving, of praying, and of allowing the gifts of the Spirit to operate are all good works ordained by God. Through them we learn and are prepared, little by little, for His eternal purpose, the image of Jesus.

The trials and testings of life, the struggles and daily challenges we face, the heartbreaks and the victories are all part of God's hand at work in my life and in your life. If we focus only on the "planet earth" experiences, we may become discouraged and confused, for they vary depending upon the eternal work God is seeking to accomplish. As a builder uses many different tools to accomplish his goal, and a painter uses many different colors to produce his masterpiece, so God uses many different experiences to move us toward His ultimate predestined purpose for our lives. Some of the names on God's tools could be suffering, adversity, sickness, hardship, victory and blessing.

Ephesians speaks more about our predetermined destiny in God. We are predestined to be His adopted children (Eph. 1:5). We are not orphans for all eternity! Though our earthly parents die, yet we are not without God as our Father. We have been adopted by Jesus Christ into the eternal, loving, glorious family of God. In Verse 11, we are told that it is predetermined that we receive an inheritance. This is no meager portion either! We have an eternal inheritance in the riches and glories of the Creator of all things. Not only are we adopted and saved from orphanhood, but we have been chosen by a very wealthy and prosperous Father. Glory to God! The thought of receiving an inheritance of substantial wealth is quite exciting. We envision how our life would change, what we would do with the money, and how happy we would be. How much more we have to be thankful for, as we realize that our destiny includes an inheritance of wealth beyond our wildest dreams. We have been adopted into a family that was not accessible to us until we were saved from our sins by the great love of God.

As wonderful as this life is at times, particularly when in the blessed presence of the Spirit of God, there is yet a Scripture that speaks to the far greater blessedness of what is to come in the vast and endless ages of eternity. In Romans 13:12, we are told that we are in the "night" of our experience, and that the day is soon to dawn. Paul likewise explained that now we see through a glass darkly, but then shall we see face to face and know as we are known (I Cor. 13:12). In the night, before the sun rises, objects are not very clear. We see shadows, shapes and broad generalities, but the details escape us. Colors are muted or nondistinguishable. We cannot fully enjoy the landscape of our surroundings for there is not enough light. Then comes the sun. All of a sudden we see shapes clearly. Colors that previously were darkened burst to life. The cool of the night is dispelled with the warmth of the sun's rays. Day has arrived! What a glorious thought to realize that this is our "nighttime" experience, and the day is soon to dawn. Soon the rays of the Son of God will brighten our existence and we will see colors, shapes and a landscape of glory of which, heretofore, we have only had a glimpse.

What glorious love God has for us! He sent His Son, Jesus, to die on the cross, shed His blood for our atonement, and rise from the dead as the firstborn of many into eternal life. This love, shown to us through Jesus, is the love that predestined us to be His children and share in the inheritance of His riches for all eternity. It is in this life that He seeks to prepare us for our destiny! It is coming, and He wants us prepared. Children who inherit great wealth, but have no strength of character, are often destroyed by the power of what they receive. God intends for the Christian to be prepared for his destiny and have the character of Christ, to be able to fully enjoy the inheritance. He knows just what each of us needs to experience to be fitted for this plan. As we learn to lift our eyes to the horizons of God's predetermined purpose, we will receive the strength to endure all of the "work" taking place in our lives. As Paul put it, "Our conversation (citizenship) is in heaven" (Phil 3:20).

Our efforts should be focused upon obtaining God's purpose, not our own. Paul explained that his goal was to seize and possess that which God purposed for him in Christ Jesus. Because this was his focus, what befell him in this life was of little importance to Paul. He pressed on to reach the fullness of the high calling of God in his life. He sought to align himself with the eternal purposes of God. As we seek to do the same, all of heaven will move to help us. When we seek to move into that which God has predetermined, we move into the flow of eternity and a taste of our glorious inheritance. His goal is to make us more like Jesus (Phil. 3:12-15).

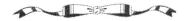

Also Available from Spirit of Truth Publications...

Strengthening The Spiritual Man

Lex W. Adams
Lynn M. Adams

For the Christian who desires to focus on Jesus amidst the many influences which attempt to hinder his relationship with God.

ISBN 0-9643206-1-4

Inquire at your local Christian Bookstore

or you may order from

Spirit of Truth Publications
P. O. Box 2979
Minden, NV 89423

Spirit of Truth Publications

TREASURES FOR THE HEART

A Collection of Inspirational Teachings and Prayers

April, 1995

Dear Friends in Christ,

Enclosed is a complimentary copy of our new book. We pray you will find the contents a blessing and of benefit in your walk with the Lord. The chapters are a compilation of writings over the past five years originating from our periodical "Spirit of Truth" letters. We began this project approximately one year ago with the whole family helping in one area or another. We hope you enjoy the results.

If you, or anyone you know, would like to order additional copies, you may do so by writing Spirit of Truth Publications, P.O. Box 2979, Minden, NV 89423. The price is $7.95 each, plus $1 shipping and handling. For orders of six or more shipping and handling is free.

May the Lord bless you and keep you until the glorious day of His coming.

Sincerely in Christ,

Lex & Lynn Adams

Lex & Lynn Adams • P.O. Box 2979 • Minden, Nevada 89423